Saltwater Taffy and Red High Heels

Salt Water Taffy and Red High Heels:
My Journey through Breast Cancer
A memoir by Crystal Brown-Tatum

Saltwater Taffy and Red High Heels

Pray for one another, that you may be healed.
James 5: 16

Acknowledgments

When you are in the midst of a storm, you feel like you are suffocating and will drown. The sunshine is imminent but while it rains, it's hard to imagine anything but the current dreary state. Words can not express how much the prayers, letters, cards, emails, gifts and sentiments meant to me during my treatment; especially after my surgery when I was in extreme pain and barely able to move or function normally.

Thank you to my wonderful sister-in-law Karen Gilder, who happens to be an oncology registered nurse, for her encouragement and guidance during my initial diagnosis and subsequent treatments. I think I emailed her everyday while preparing for chemo!

Thank you to my mother, Margaret Brown and brother Alton Tatum, who are also registered nurses, for their unconditional love and financial support while I recovered. I know it was hard for my mom seeing me go through this but I pray she finds comfort in knowing that she is the greatest source of my strength.

Thank you to my "chemo buddy" and sister in the struggle Mindy Armstead. Our daily emails really meant a lot to me and together, we were invincible. I am so glad that Evelyn Flores and Terri Hornsby made the connection for us.

Thank you to my medical team-Dr. Kevin Marler, Dr. Joyce Feagin and Dr. Sanford Katz-for their expertise, encouragement and professionalism. Their guidance made each step on the journey a little easier and I gained confidence under their care. A resounding "thank you" and round of applause to the entire staff at the Willis Knighton Cancer Center in Shreveport, Louisiana. It's one thing to come to work and just do your job but it's another to do your job well done and enjoy what you do!

My lifelong and new friends who contributed to this book and read countless emails and viewed more surgical photos than they desired-"Thank you" and I love you from the bottom of my heart.

My newfound friends in Shreveport-Twana Jackson, Jackie Young, Ginevra Collins, Danielle Jones, Paula Garlock, Linda Dotie, Kathie Rowell, Mary Moore and LaShanna Winters-for their kind-hearted gestures and Christian love.

Saltwater Taffy and Red High Heels

Thank you to Houston's elite-First Lady Andrea White and Attorneys Sofia Adrogue and Marcy Kurtz-for your kind notes of encouragement and putting me in touch with other strong, successful women who encouraged me often on this walk.

Thank you to the American Cancer Society for the valuable services and resources they extended to me. They made me "feel good and look better!"

Thank you to Karen Jackson of Sisters Network for always making yourself available and for all that you for women fighting this disease. You are a walking testimony and inspiration more than you know.

Thank you to Sandy Lawrence-the hardest working woman in the literary field. Your family has embraced me like one of their own and I appreciate and love you very much.

Thank you to attorney Ella Brown-McCoy for your professional guidance during a challenging episode.

Thank you to my incarcerated friends who prayed for me daily and sent letters of encouragement and friendship. The world may judge you but I know the goodness in your heart.

Thank you to my husband Phil who quite possibly saved my life by urging me to go to the Dr. and providing me with health insurance. Thank you for putting up with my mood swings and sharp tongue when chemo got the best of me. You are the best and I love you very much.

My daughter Jackie who always gives me motivation to fight hard and excel in every endeavor taken. I pray that this is one journey that you will never have to take but I know that you have that survivor spirit in you and will be fine. Please know that I have always put you first.

And last but not least, my dog Cotton-quite possibly the world's best dog! On my worst chemo days, he would crawl into bed and keep me

Saltwater Taffy and Red High Heels

company. On my good days, he would try on my wigs! One bark says it all.

Saltwater Taffy and Red High Heels

<u>Milestones</u>

1. The Beginning
2. Momo's Breast Cancer
3. The Lump
4. First Dr. Visit
5. Getting the News
6. The First Week
7. Keeping A Breast of the Situation
8. Chemo From Head to Toe
9. Hair Today, Gone Tomorrow
10. Goodness Radiates
11. Angels Among Us
12. The Surgery
13. Ups and Downs, Highs and Lows
14. Reflections

The Beginning

There I was. March 24th, 2007 outside of Ashford United Methodist Church in Houston, Texas. I nervously sat in the limo while the bridal party marched down the aisle awaiting my grand debut. My special day had finally arrived…my wedding day. I honestly thought that all of my dreams would come true and that all of my heartaches and major obstacles were a thing of the past. Little did I know that cancer was also in this picture. And so it begins.

Saltwater Taffy and Red High Heels

Momo's Breast Cancer

We affectionately called my maternal grandmother "Momo." She is the only grandparent that I have had a lifetime meaningful relationship with. My mother's father passed away when I was in middle school and my father lost his parents when he was a child. Momo was the nucleus and pillar of a sometimes dysfunctional family. If you look up grandmother in the dictionary, you should see her photograph. She was that special and dear to me.

My daughter Jaclyn and Momo-Christmas 2005

It was a rainy day in Houston and I was on my lunch hour. At the time, I was working for an oil and gas equipment manufacturing firm and was under close watch to keep my lunch hour at 59 minutes! I remember the phone call as if it was yesterday. I was sitting in my car in a TGI Friday's parking lot, dodging the rain and trying to protect my hairstyle, when my mom called to tell me the news. I held my bright pink cell phone closely to my ear.

"Momo has breast cancer", she sobbed. I was stung and at a complete loss for words. My grandmother was 80 years old! How could this be? Was this even possible? Are they sure it was breast cancer? We both cried for what seemed like an eternity. For me, the word cancer was a death sentence at that time. Sure, I wore a pink ribbon lapel pin in October and even donated to various breast cancer foundations but I really did not know that much about the disease except that it seemed to rob women of everything that contributed to their femininity (hair, breasts, eyelashes, etc.)

My mother's best friend, whom I affectionately called Aunt Norma over the years, died from breast cancer when I was a teenager. Other than that, I had never personally known anyone who had or died from breast cancer but I was very familiar with the term and the national efforts to find a cure through walk-a-thons, races, etc. In fact, when I thought of women with breast cancer, I would mentally reference older, Caucasian women. Never in a million years would I think that I would have breast cancer someday but once I was diagnosed, my thinking changed to why not me? Who am I to be spared from this disease that affects so many others? My journey will be no different than the woman who has traveled this path before me.

Saltwater Taffy and Red High Heels

Needless to say, the rest of the work day was terrible. I shared the news with my coworkers who were sympathetic and then I went home and cried some more. When I broke the news to my daughter Jaclyn, who was nine years old at the time, we hugged and cried on her bed. My grandmother was always one of the strongest women I have ever known. She was a quiet but proud woman who lived alone (twice widowed) in one of the most impoverished areas of San Antonio, Texas. After thirty plus years, she retired from being a nursing assistant in a local nursing home. In fact, she rarely missed a day of work and worked hard for a low hourly wage.

I have very fond memories of my grandmother. I can recall how her home smelled, that her favorite perfumes were Giorgio Red and Imari by Avon, and how she would feed the neighborhood cats. She was always the comfort after the storm in my childhood.

Momo had a mastectomy. Apparently, the cancer had been in her body a long time. I guess she was uncomfortable talking about her breasts and or having another person touch them! According to my mother, by the time she finally got around to showing my mother the suspicious lump, it was very large, hard and even had a foul smell to it.

Since I lived in Houston, I wasn't able to be there for any of her treatments or surgery but I do know from my mother that she came through everything with flying colors and the courage of a soldier. I was amazed at how fast her recovery was and how she was able to return back to an independent lifestyle in a few weeks.

Saltwater Taffy and Red High Heels

From my personal recollection, my grandmother always lived alone for the exception of being married to a man that died when I was very young. She ate at the same time everyday and watched the same television shows everyday for 35+ years! "The Price is Right", "Young and the Restless," "Wheel of Fortune" and "Guiding Light" were among her favorites. She was a smoker in my early childhood and rumor has it that she drank too although I don't recall her doing either. Since I was born with chronic asthma, she never smoked around me since she kept me most weekends while my parents worked.

I remember seeing Momo for the first time post-mastectomy. She didn't look any different and her chest appeared normal. I would later learn that she wore a prosthetic bra. I was very nervous to hug her from that point on and hugged her from the side. Much to my pleasant surprise, nothing had really changed. She was still the best grandmother in the whole wide world!

We never really talked about the cancer or surgery. She did express to me on one occasion that her medication was expensive but other than that, her daily routine went on as usual. Sadly, she passed away five years later at the age of 85. I wish she were here with me on my own journey of survival. I know she would have something funny to offer or just a shoulder to cry on. Part of me feels that she would be sad or guilty because most likely, I got the disease from her. If I could spend one more day with her, I would tell her that the most important things I got from her were strength, compassion, independence and a survival mechanism that kicks in at the earliest sign of attack!

Like most breast cancer patients, I have asked why and questioned my lifestyle habits in search of a reason. Was it my high fat diet? Was it the birth control pills that I took in my youth? Was it my lack of a routine exercise regimen? Was it the stress of my job? Was it payback for prior sins committed? Why did breast cancer skip a generation and why doesn't my mom have it? Will my daughter have it? After you get past the "sleuth" stage, you realize that regardless of why you got breast cancer, you must accept your diagnosis, educate yourself on the treatment options and quickly move forward to treatment and recovery.

Saltwater Taffy and Red High Heels

The Lump

I remember lying across the bed in August 2006 with my new boyfriend and my now husband Philip. We had attended college together sixteen years ago at The University of Houston. Back in college, we would pass each other in the dorm and were acquainted with the same circle of friends but no sparks ever flew. When our paths would cross again, the timing was right for us to fall in love. I had been looking for Mr. Right for so long and even took my search nationally by being featured in Ebony magazine as a Top Bachelorette. I honestly thought that I would find my future husband through postal mail correspondence but I now believe that God puts people in our lives at the right time for the right reasons. You have to have your eyes wide open so that you can realize it.

I was applying lotion to my body after a shower and felt an odd round lump that I had never felt in my armpit area before. It was hard, moveable and the size of a small marble. I had experienced similar enlarged nodes in my neck area that went away in a few days so I really didn't think much of it at the time. Although the lump didn't hurt, Phil said I should have it looked at by a doctor. My initial response was that it was an allergic reaction to a new deodorant or a swollen lymph node due to my chronic sinusitis. I am a highly allergic individual who takes antihistamines like Altoids!

Saltwater Taffy and Red High Heels

Over the next few months, I became completely obsessed with that lump; often feeling it and "messin' with it" as Phil would say. It was like I actually thought that "messin' with it" would make it go away. I even tried to massage it down and crush it frequently. I guess you could say I was overly obsessed with my body and any perceived imperfection would haunt me!

On Christmas Day, 2006, I had my mother, brother, and sister-in-law, who are all registered nurses, look at it and examine it. They dismissed it as a cyst or fatty tumor although my sister-in-law (the oncology nurse) suggested I go to the doctor as soon as possible. My mother had a similarly sized benign fatty tumor removed from her arm so that reassured me for a while. My sister-in-law would later tell me that her initial response to herself was "Oh crap!"….well, not exactly those family friendly words. I even emailed a friend of mine, Kelly, who works for a national breast cancer organization about getting a free mammogram. Her advice to me was to be seen by a doctor right away and not to let too much time pass. She took my lump more seriously than I did. I NEVER even gave it a thought that it could be breast cancer. I just wanted this knot out of my body.

There is truth to the phrase: "Out of sight, out of mind." Phil and I got engaged in December and I actively planned the wedding of my dreams in March 2007. I confidently bought a strapless wedding gown of my dreams on my first wedding dress shopping trip! Not once did I even worry about that underarm lump even though I knew I would have my arms above my head throughout the day. My biggest concern was keeping that underarm fresh and free of white residue! Once again, after the wedding, I became even more obsessed with the lump and would lie in bed feeling it. I guess this is the time for me to let you know that I am a compulsive obsessive type A personality. I'm one of those people who just knows when my body is not in tune and I like for everything to be in balance. My zodiac sign is Libra and I guess that is why I have to have things in order and balanced. My daughter would catch me touching it and would tell me to stop and that it wasn't cancer. "You're so dramatic", she would tease. She's a teenager so trust me, she knows drama!

Looking back, so many people told me that it wasn't cancer that I may have bought into that had Momo not been diagnosed with the disease. It was as if no one wanted to believe that I could be a cancer candidate. Eventually, I was able to get Phil's concurrence that "it" was getting larger and if I laid in a certain position, it began to be uncomfortable. Despite my deepest subconscious fear, it was time to see a doctor. I had waited way too long.

Another reason that I was reluctant to go to the doctor was because I didn't have health insurance prior to getting married. Yes, I was a successful entrepreneur but the premiums for health coverage were outrageous and since my asthma and allergies were pre-existing conditions, I just couldn't justify paying money for a plan that wouldn't cover my major medical concerns. It is important for me to say this because so many people don't have health insurance and it is a shame. People who don't have health insurance can be just like me: educated, goal-oriented and hard-working. The reality is that if I waited another year or two, my cancer may have metastasized and possibly been Stage 4 when diagnosed. If you get anything out of reading my memoir, please get this: IF THERE IS ANYTHING SUSPICIOUS IN YOUR BREAST AREA, GET TO A DOCTOR ASAP! Don't play around with your health. I made time for everyone else but didn't make time to go to the doctor.

Throughout this journey, I was amazed at how many women would ask me if they could feel the lump or shared that they had similar lumps that they quickly dismissed as swollen glands. It is critical that women "get over the lump" and see a physician about anything suspicious in the breast area. While writing this book, I was also surprised at how many women confided in me that they had a lump in their breast area but because of lack of health insurance, they hadn't gone to the doctor yet.

It is reassuring that women can open up and be inquisitive about this disease. We wouldn't hesitate to show an arm lesion and we must not be embarrassed about asking breast questions. Half of the time, we are throwing them in each other's faces anyway through cleavage baring tops or swim suits!

For me, FEAR is Forced Exclusions Are Ridiculous! Fear paralyzed me for going to the doctor sooner. Deep down, I wasn't

Saltwater Taffy and Red High Heels

prepared for a malignant biopsy in any capacity-emotionally, spiritually or financially.

One of my closest friends had this to say when I asked her how she felt when I told her of my diagnosis:

Being your Matron of Honor was a proud and humbling moment for me. I've always admired you and the best and brightest have always been drawn to you. So, I felt honored that you chose me to share your most special day. I'd seen you go through so much heartbreak, trying to be strong, but still wanting a shoulder to lean on when things got tough. You have endured many things. Spending time with you and Phil during the wedding, I felt a sense of calm. All those years, through all the disappointments, I had always promised that you would find that special person who was worthy of you, and who accepted you for all the things that you are, and all the things you have been through. Your day had arrived and I knew it was the beginning of everything you had always hoped for.

When you told me about the doctor's reaction during your exam, I was in denial. I told myself that it could not be cancer and wouldn't allow myself to think about it. Not now, not when you had already endured so much in life to get to this place of happiness. You hadn't even had time to unpack your wedding gifts! I was leaving a professional development class when I got your text message that cancer had been confirmed. There was shock, then tears as I pulled out of the Rice University parking lot. I called you and we talked. For the first time I thought, "I can't imagine life without Crystal Brown."

Since that day, I have learned so much through you. And I continue to admire your courage and strength. You were put here to inspire others and touch their lives in a way that no one else can. And, I am confident that you are bigger than this disease. Nothing, disease, loss of hair, treatments, past disappointments, NOTHING, is bigger than your smile and your heart. You always have been a survivor, and I'm praying that this time will be no different.

Saltwater Taffy and Red High Heels

I've seen a stronger, more beautiful, Crystal. You are sure of yourself in a way that you never have been before. When you e-mailed your picture with the bald head and no wig, I said, "This is a new, very brave women . . . because I can remember a time when you would have been too insecure to shave your head, and then show everybody!" That told me that you were ready to fight, and ready to win. The little bushy-headed girl with the red hair from UH has grown into a self-assured, sophisticated woman. Cancer better watch out, damn the statistics, because you have beaten the odds many times before.

Mrs. *Shelia-Redmon Jones*

The author and Shelia-Redmon Jones on 3/24/07

And the odds were once again in my favor.

Saltwater Taffy and Red High Heels

First Doctor Visit

Let me stress again how good it feels to FINALLY have health insurance after years of no coverage! After my corporate layoff from a very large and well known software developer, I couldn't afford to pay a COBRA premium of $900 a month for my daughter and I. I practically waltzed into that doctor's office on Thursday, April 19, 2007 and if you know me personally, you can easily imagine that waltz! Over the years, I had incurred enough out of pocket expenses to make me steer away from the doctor's office. Since I am allergic to penicillin, my antibiotic choices are limited and would often cost me more than $200 out of pocket plus a $75 office visit. I remember asking myself on several occasions "How long can I put off feeling sick verse spending $300 on an office visit today?" My heart sincerely goes out to people without access to healthcare. It just doesn't seem fair that some people have wellness and others don't.

I filled out the lengthy new patient paperwork and sat back down to finish a "Good Housekeeping" article. You can tell a lot about a doctor's personality by the magazines he or she keeps in their waiting area. Let's see…Oprah, Sports Illustrated, Good Housekeeping, Vogue. I had surmised that the doctor was well rounded, diverse and warm. If anything, he had enough common sense to know how to order good lobby area magazines!

Saltwater Taffy and Red High Heels

I had been referred to this surgeon over the phone by another OB/GYN practitioner. I was new to the area and was hand picking physicians out of the provider directory on the sound of their name alone. Not always a good idea but at least I'm honest! I appreciated that the OB/GYN did not waste my time and office visit by sending me directly to the oncology surgeon for an evaluation.

Boy did I luck out! Dr. Kevin Marler was patient oriented, friendly, handsome and had a voice just like Matthew McConnaughey! His office staff was friendly and he immediately put me at ease with his Southern charm, professional demeanor and attentiveness without rushing the appointment. He really seemed to know how to manage patients who were facing possible cancer diagnosis because his approach was direct without being abrasive. We made small talk as he examined my left breast and I caution you here: it is never easy to hold a decent conversation while a physician has his hands on your breast! No matter how cute he is! When he got to the lump, his demeanor changed and he took on a more serious tone. He told the nurse to go get the ultrasound machine and a knot formed in my stomach. I hadn't had an ultrasound since I was ten weeks pregnant with my daughter and didn't really understand what was going on.

Initially, because of my smaller breast size (34B-thank you very much!), he thought that it would not be a cancerous lump because he felt a lot of tissue density. He showed me the lump on the monitor and it was approximately 1.74 cm. Because it appeared clear, I had a false sense of security that it was a just a cyst but when he asked me what I was doing tomorrow, I knew he didn't want dinner and a movie. He wanted me to return for a biopsy the next afternoon.

Isn't it funny that you can hear a word over your lifetime and never truly know what it means? I had heard biopsy a million times but never took the time to research it. Like most of you, I headed home and typed in biopsy in google. As we like to say in my house, "I googled it." When did google became a verb?

I was terrified at the search engine results! The doctor was going to stick a long needle under my arm and into my breast area while I was awake? Are you for real? I was so scared and apprehensive about the procedure that he prescribed a valium to take one hour before I came in.

Phil accompanied me to the procedure. I knew that having him with me would make me stronger. I mean, who wants to have a complete mental breakdown and hissy fit in front of their new husband? The doctor numbed the area and demonstrated what the clicking noise would be that would soon follow. Now I am a big crybaby when it comes to medical procedures but I have learned, especially after NATURAL childbirth, that if you can breathe deeply and focus on something other than the pain in the moment, you can tolerate it. Maybe watching the "Saw" and "Scream" movie trilogies helped desensitize me to pain and torture.

Saltwater Taffy and Red High Heels

I didn't really feel the needle going in but I squeezed Phil's hand tightly. I was more worried about how my underarm smelled than the actual needle. When the needle met the tissue, you would hear a click and that was slightly painful. The biopsy didn't take long and wasn't as bad as the internet made it sound. My sister-in-law, the great oncology nurse, reminded me that most of the information on the internet pertaining to health is outdated. As patients, we need to realize that not everything you google is gold.

The next day, I had minimal bruising and soreness around the biopsy site. The small entry holes were also visible but nothing to scoff at. I had survived the fearful biopsy but could have never been prepared for the test results.

Saltwater Taffy and Red High Heels

Getting the News

I have been actively involved with the American Heart Association (AHA) for several years in a volunteer capacity. The strength of any nonprofit organization is in their volunteers. I lost my father in 1991 due to heart disease when he was only fifty four years old and I was nineteen. Losing my father greatly impacted my life and my involvement with AHA to help prevent or lessen deaths from heart disease and stroke is my father's legacy in motion. Since my breast cancer diagnosis, I have questioned whether my energy and efforts will be better served for a cancer non-profit organization. You can support a cause all your life but until YOU are personally affected, I don't think you can fully champion it.

Although Dr. Marler, Phil and I agreed to wait until Wednesday to discuss the results since I would be in Washington, D.C. Monday through Wednesday morning, I decided to call the office on Tuesday afternoon after completing my congressional visits. In hindsight, I don't know why I subjected myself to that phone call prematurely but I am known for being stubborn. Imagine that- a stubborn Southern woman! Perhaps I was overly confident that the news would be positive. I kept thinking that there was no way I could have breast cancer.

Saltwater Taffy and Red High Heels

Me about 2 hours before receiving my diagnosis.

I was on a shuttle bus with AHA advocates from various states. Luckily, some of my fellow Texas delegates were on the bus; particularly one woman, who happens to be a registered nurse, whom I had befriended who had shared with me the previous evening that she was a one-year colon cancer survivor. Ann had already inspired me with her courage and she was someone I had always admired from afar for her beauty and intelligence. Since I come from a family of registered nurses, I have a deep respect for nurses.

 Now keep in mind, my stubbornness. When the nurse got on the phone, she informed that the doctor wasn't in and I was like "so?" She said that this is the part of her job that she hates. When she told me it was cancer, everything around me stopped. I felt frozen.

Saltwater Taffy and Red High Heels

I think I must have asked her to repeat herself three of four times. I was fortunate to be seated across from Ann and I literally jumped over to her seat and cried on her shoulder.

Hearing "you have cancer" can be one of the most heart rendering experiences anyone can go through. I know, as I was diagnosed with colon cancer in August of 2006 and under went eight months of chemotherapy. I had just finished my treatments when I joined Crystal and the AHA folks in Washington, DC. I truly believe that things happen to us for a reason- we may not understand it at the time- but there is a master plan out there. When Crystal first told me she may have breast cancer and was waiting for the doctor to call her, I shared with her my story. Each time you speak of cancer, your cancer, out loud, it gets easier.

I know how difficult it was for me to hear those words and could only imagine what Crystal was going through when her doctor told her—we were on the bus coming back from the capital. We cried. We hugged. We knew how scary this was. But we had each other and I am glad Crystal didn't have to be alone. "
Ann Quinn Todd, RN, MSN, CNA-BC, FAHA

When I got back in my room, I cried some more. I had held it together until I was safe behind closed doors. Over the years, I had mastered the ability to hold my emotions in and put a very different front to the outside world and there has only been one person that could see right through that facade and see the real me. Thank you Linda Blume.

The walk from the shuttle bus, through the hotel lobby, up the elevator and to my room seemed like a thousand miles. The first person I wanted to call was my mother but I couldn't get in touch with her. I knew she would be devastated by the news. I was able to reach my "other mother", my mother-in-law, who comforted me and asked me not to tell my husband until I got home. She knew that he would be heartbroken by the results. It was so hard speaking to him that evening and not breaking down. He was headed to a softball game and I didn't want to take joy from him; my news would have to wait. He sounded so happy to hear from me and it pained my heart deeply to have to tell him that his new wife had breast cancer. One of the hardest things to do is to tell your loved ones that you have cancer.

I couldn't stand just sitting in the hotel room and Sanjaya was still on American Idol, so I went for a walk to get some fresh air. Retail therapy. It always works for me! I remembered seeing Macy's a few blocks away while leaving for the Capitol that morning. As I walked down the street, everything seemed so different. I felt that everyone could look at me and knew I was ill. I know it sounds ridiculous but that is how I felt.

I walked into Macy's and the shoe department was the first area I came into. I walked around the area; perusing all of the red shoes in stock. I had been wanting; craving is a better word, some red high heels for the longest. Jessica Simspon looks great in them! So does Cameron Diaz and Eva Longoria. So, why did I want a pair for so long but never indulged?

Which brings me to the title of this memoir: Salt Water Taffy and Red High Heels. I'll discuss the taffy in a minute. Buying those red

Saltwater Taffy and Red High Heels

patent leather Rampage high heels instantly made me feel better. They were sexy, fun, stylish, eye-catching…everything I always hoped to be. I told myself that if I needed chemotherapy or radiation, I would arrive in style! Yes, I would show up to my appointments in those damn red high heels! I even envisioned different outfits I could wear: black and white striped sweater, white pants, red shoes or maybe a black cocktail dress with red shoes.

Women are funny creatures. Don't look around as if this doesn't apply to you! You know we are. We fight over men but connect over shoes. I met several nice women that evening at Macy's, shared a few laughs and even looked at baby pictures! One woman in particular befriended me and encouraged me to walk down the street to another shoe store in my quest for a great pair of red shoes. After all, if I was going to kick cancer's butt, I should have on great shoes! We walked down the street laughing like we were old friends; even sharing our children's photos! My quest finally ended back at Macy's where I bought the much anticipated red shoes. Looking back, I don't know how I held it together emotionally long enough to make a new friend and a new shoe purchase but buying those much anticipated red shoes empowered me. I could take control of what I wanted. Despite my circumstances, I could choose to be happy. I could control my destiny.

Saltwater Taffy and Red High Heels

When I started radiation, I was pleasantly surprised to receive a phone call from Sherrill, the woman I had met at Macy's that dreaded evening. She told me that she had thought of me often and was so happy that I was doing well. She even went home that evening and told her husband how she met a young woman who was so strong after learning she had cancer. Sherrill said she didn't think she would have held it together as well as I did after receiving the diagnosis. I often wonder how I manage to be strong in the most challenging of circumstances but somehow, I do what I need to do. I encourage you to do the same.

Word of my diagnosis quickly spread to the AHA committee members that evening. We had all adjourned to our hotel rooms by late afternoon. Our Board Chairman's wife called me and asked if I wanted company. We met in the cocktail club over tea and it was so nice to have her to talk to. I think I consumed four spring rolls, bread pudding, two chocolate chip cookies and then some! We shared so many tears and laughs in that room. I know that sometimes people don't know what to say; it doesn't mean that they don't care or that they are not thinking about you. They may simply not KNOW what to say. One thing you can offer a woman with a new diagnosis is the gift of listening. You don't have to know the "right" words to say. You can be a sounding board for her fears and questions.

Saltwater Taffy and Red High Heels

I guess what initially brought me to you was Gary. He introduced us at dinner and immediately I liked you! From there, you and I talked about women, depression, children, etc. and you just exuded that warmth and strength that you do, so I was thinking to myself, "This is so nice to meet a real person that isn't afraid to open up to me and put herself out there". But it did not take me long to realize that God's hand was all over this meeting. Once I came upstairs (to that cool suite) we talked about the options, possibilities, support available, worst case scenarios, everything! I felt privileged to be there with you during that time. I had not met anyone before you who had gone
through this personally, so I was glad to be there for you in whatever capacity that meant to you. Throughout the year I have watched you from a distance handle this life event with all of the grace, style, and endurance that I am certain you have handled everything else in your life with. You still surprise me though! You are awesome and inspiring!
Mrs. Carole Hall

On my flight back to Shreveport, I was walking around the Atlanta airport (Man, is that airport huge!) trying not to break down and cry. It is surreal to keep news like that to yourself and not to share it with your closest loved ones. I was lucky enough to have been seated next to a very intellectual man who was a bank president on the flight from D.C. and we engaged in conversation which kept my mind off of the diagnosis. I recall discussing rap music and the hip hop genre and how it affects our youth. That's pretty heavy conversation for an airplane ride! It would have been awful for me to have a breakdown on the plane and I am certain security or Air Marshalls would have showed up to escort me off the plane.

Saltwater Taffy and Red High Heels

I have a ritual of collecting shot glasses from every city that I visit so I walked into one of the gift shops to purchase a souvenir glass. Now, that same frugality that held me back from the red shoes previously, attempted to creep back in the picture when I saw a bag of Georgia Salt Water Taffy. I have always loved salt water taffy but not everyone makes good taffy. No, Laffy Taffy is NOT real taffy. Normally the $4.99 price tag would have sent me packing but things were different for me now. As a single mother for thirteen years, I had trained myself not to splurge on myself or spend money on things that I really didn't need. Not like the 120 pairs of shoes I own though! I really need those! I would no longer deny myself any affordable or reasonable indulgence. I really enjoyed that bag of taffy piece by piece. I hid them in a kitchen drawer and would treat myself to one as a snack or desert daily. I have come to realize that life is really too short to miss out on the small and simple indulgences. I am not advocating financial hardships or big purchases to make you feel better but don't wait until it is too late to fully enjoy everything you want out of life!

When Crystal asked me to write down what were my initial thoughts after I found out about her breast cancer diagnosis I was a bit hesitant, because my first thoughts were anything but positive or uplifting. I believe when one writes, they need to write honestly in order to be successful, and I knew if I were going to be honest, it would reveal me as the eternal pessimist I have always been ashamed to be. Not something I really wanted to do, so I just put the request on the "back burner", knowing God would eventually put the words in my heart, and now He has.

Saltwater Taffy and Red High Heels

I've known Crystal since grade school, so I know first-hand that she has faced pain and struggle the majority of her life. Losing her father the way she did and dealing with her family issues are only the tip of the iceberg. She was a little girl, I believe, filled with anger and insecurity, masked by a whole heap of attitude and defensive behavior. She was beautiful and popular, but, because of this, definitely experienced her share of problems with peers and teachers. Her and I even had our battles at times. She experienced true heartbreak and love lost at just 13, and I don't think she ever really recovered from that until well until adulthood. She survived broken heart after broken heart and failed relationship after failed relationship. In the meantime, she struggled as a single mother and a black woman in the work force. Then, finally, it seemed things were looking up. Her business was thriving and she had finally found true, reliable love. Consequently, when Crystal told me she had breast cancer, my first thought was, "Geez! If Crystal didn't have bad luck, she wouldn't have any luck at all! I wondered what on Earth has this poor girl done to deserve this?!? Hasn't she been through enough?!?"

But, then something remarkable happened – I saw Crystal evolving into the woman God always intended her to be. More than that, I realized Crystal was truly blessed. She's been blessed with the grace of perseverance. The struggles I pitied her for have, in fact, been blessings disguised, because they have made her so strong. She's a go-getter. She's a mover and a shaker. She's a SURVIVOR. Her struggles have led her to remarkable accomplishments and once-of-a-lifetime experiences. And, most importantly, she's blessed with dozens of friends who look up to her and truly care about her and truly love her. Crystal, your life is a testament to God's love for us and an example of how we should all act and live when faced with hardship.

Mrs. Anna Dinkins

Saltwater Taffy and Red High Heels

The First Week

By the time I arrived home, Phil was a nervous wreck. I can only imagine how hard the news must have been for him and how unfair it must have seemed. In hindsight, I wish I would have waited to tell him in person. Just as receiving the news over the phone packed a punch for me, I delivered a similar blow to Phil and I regret that. His tears and cries on the phone were earth shattering. Some of his military colleagues even came out to the house to sit with him before I returned. News of cancer has the ability to knock one off their feet.

The first week felt like I was living in a dream. Every morning, I metaphorically pinched myself to see if this was all a long, bad dream. I had to fight back the urge to cry whenever I spoke the "c-word." It just didn't seem fair to my husband that he married the "girl of his dreams" and a month later, she was diagnosed with breast cancer. Besides telling Phil, telling my thirteen year-old daughter I had breast cancer was difficult. Jaclyn had seen me very ill and hospitalized with asthma on many occasions but this was different. This was cancer.

I waited until after school to talk to her. I walked in her room, sat on her bed and took a deep breath. Before I could get it out, she bravely said "I already know. I had a dream last night that you told me you had breast cancer." We hugged and cried and then she asked me if she could go ride her bike. Teenagers are an interesting species and they choose to deal with things on their own terms and in their own time. In hindsight, I would have to say that Jaclyn was very strong and brave throughout my ordeal. I made myself available for questions but she really didn't want to talk about it. She would ask me often if I was in pain or needed anything. I really don't think she ever accepted that I could possibly die from this disease.

My mom was in denial in the early stages of my diagnosis. She questioned why I had it but she didn't. She was also concerned that I had gone from one emotional high to an emotional low. It just didn't seem fair. I had a brother who was dealing with a serious medical emergency around the same time and mom felt like she was being pulled in so many directions.

It wasn't so hard telling my closest friends, loved ones and clients. My life has always been an open book. Sometimes, sharing has come back to bite me in the butt but it hasn't stolen my spirit to share. We grow from learning about the mistakes that others before us have made. E-mail communication made that dialogue much easier for me. Several people immediately called me but most emailed a response back. I imagine it is awkward to receive such an email but I couldn't possibly pick up the phone and have the "cancer" conversation with 50 or so people.

All of my clients were understanding and supportive. I have worked hard to build a successful public relations business, with myself being the top client, and it saddened me to think that all of

Saltwater Taffy and Red High Heels

my hard work may go down the drain with the news that I was ill. I actually went the extra mile to assure people that I was still competent and well enough to work. During chemotherapy, I still wrote press releases and media alerts, planned special events, wrote freelance articles and closed new business deals. Working was therapeutic for me as it took my mind off of the daily blahs.

I began to look at the world differently too. The little things that would normally bother me like bad drivers or long lines didn't bother me so much. I smiled more at strangers and when I commented on the weather, I honestly meant that the day was beautiful. I've always hated that people often take the simple things for granted.

I also began to have more fun when I got dressed for the day. Now I have always been a stylish fashionista but I had so many brooches, necklaces, and other jewelry that I rarely wore. Moving forward, EVERYDAY was going to be a special occasion. Why do we buy pretty things and only use them for special occasions? Why have pretty china but eat on mismatched dinnerware everyday? Why do we have candles on display collecting dust? Burn those darn candles! I began to face the new morning with a bright outlook and killer accessories to match.

My husband Phil loves me in a t-shirt, sweatpants and bare feet. He is one of those rare men who truly love you for who you are-battle tested and all! Although he appreciates my outward appearance, he loves strongly from his heart and made me more confident that if I

Saltwater Taffy and Red High Heels

lost my hair, lost or gain weight or had a disfigured breast, he would not treat or look at me differently. There were times that I would cover myself immediately with my bathrobe after bathing because I didn't want him to see me and start thinking about the upcoming physical changes. I had to fight back feelings of low self esteem daily as my outer beauty was being stripped away daily.

I started working out at the gym to boost my energy level and distract me from eating my emotions. To my surprise, he called me one afternoon while he was at work and said "Hey, I noticed that you are getting more toned. You look good." Phil had been consistent in wanting me to be healthy before the diagnosis and since we lived near an air force base, I could utilize the gym which offered everything under one roof.

I knew that there would be good and bad days. I knew that some days, I would feel beautiful and some days I wouldn't. I knew that my body may change for the worse. But I can face this battle with confidence because I have embraced the reality and seriousness of the situation.

I came to realize that every hardship, tragedy and obstacle that I have ever faced was only preparing me for the toughest battle of my life. People in my past who tried to hurt me only made me stronger and more self assured. All of the past anger, abuse, mistreatment and heartache memories were now minimized by my desire to persevere and conquer. It is my hope that sharing this journey will inspire you and provide comfort and strength for breast cancer patients and survivors everywhere.

Saltwater Taffy and Red High Heels

Keeping A Breast of the Situation

The morning of my lumpectomy surgery, May 10th, 2007, we had to be at the hospital at 5:30 a.m. As if it's not bad enough that you can't eat or drink after midnight! Phil and I didn't speak much while we got dressed. I think we were both scared and afraid to say the wrong thing. I woke up that morning knowing that my body would never be the same after the surgery.

Phil and I gently held hands on the drive to the hospital. He was by my side all the way into the holding area. I have to mention that the day surgery unit at Christus Schumpert hospital is the best medical facility that I have ever been a patient in. The nurses are amazing! Phil would have gone into surgery with me if the hospital would have allowed it. I just know it! In fact, he walked up to the last possible hospital approved area and the nurse had to gently tell him that he needed to go in the waiting area. She could sense his concern and sent a chaplain over to speak with him. Being wheeled into the operating room, it felt like my heart was pounding out of my chest. I knew that I would emerge from the operating room a different person forever.

I had high anxiety about my breast being disfigured and/or lopsided. Dr. Marler was such an attentive physician that he sought the permission of another patient who had undergone a mastectomy to show me her post-surgical breasts. The woman lifted her blouse and talked me through the show and tell exhibit with confidence and strength. I was amazed at how well a

Saltwater Taffy and Red High Heels

reconstructed nipple looked. "Ok, I can do this," I thought. If all failed, I could possibly get some C-cups on insurance!

I've always hated surgery. I've had three knee surgeries for a torn ACL and three sinus surgeries for nasal polyps and a deviated septum. Waking up afterwards is the worst part for me. You never know what to expect and I was afraid I would panic and hyperventilate when I woke up to the scar and tubing coming out of me. Dr. Marler had done a wonderful job of preparing me for the procedure and bringing me up to speed as far as the outcome. I had asked so many questions that I don't think I left any stone unturned.

When I woke up and was being wheeled back into my room, I remember the look of concern on Phil's face. His brother and mother had come down for support. My mother wasn't able to be there due to her own personal medical challenges at the time. Most of the first day in the hospital is a blur although I do remember violently throwing up some chicken soup that Phil was trying to feed to me. Note to self: Don't try and eat immediately after surgery!

I had a pain pump at my side which I could use to control my pain which slowly went from a lingering dull pain to a roaring giant. I slowly walked in the bathroom and looked in the mirror. The drainage tube was horrifying! It was connected to my rib cage area and had a bulb attachment that was full of bright red blood and had to be emptied every few hours. I tried to lift my arm to fix my hair

Saltwater Taffy and Red High Heels

and experienced severe shooting pain. Due to the axillary lymph node dissection, my underarm was in a lot of pain and I couldn't move my right arm very much. I had been cautioned that I may never fully use my right arm again.

Once again after surgery, Dr. Marler talked to me about chemo and I tried to tune him out. I just didn't want to lose my hair. Why was this happening to me? He informed us that once he got into the surgery, he had to remove more lymph nodes than he originally thought and they were clustered together. We would later find out that I had 16 of 27 positive lymph nodes. Basically what that means is that the cancer had entered my lymphatic system and chemotherapy would attack any remaining cancer cells in my body. I even asked an attending nurse, through a face full of fear and tears, what she would do in my shoes? She replied that if she were me, she would do all that she could and what the doctor recommended to live. She reminded me that my hair would grow back. I was honestly trying my best to talk myself out of chemotherapy and find someone who would have my back and understand my thinking at that time. I did not want chemo!

I am the type of person who is very inquisitive. I thirst for knowledge and I have a strong desire to know. So, it should come as no surprise that once I arrived home, I would peek at my surgery site before my first post-surgery office visit. Jaclyn actually fainted when she saw the drainage tube and stitches. I had never seen her faint before and it scared me to death! I mean, she literally hit the bathroom floor. Luckily, she recovered within a few minutes and popped up like "What did I miss?"

I did cry when I saw the stitches because they just looked so ugly and my body was forever scarred. My range of motion was severely impaired which limited my daily activities.

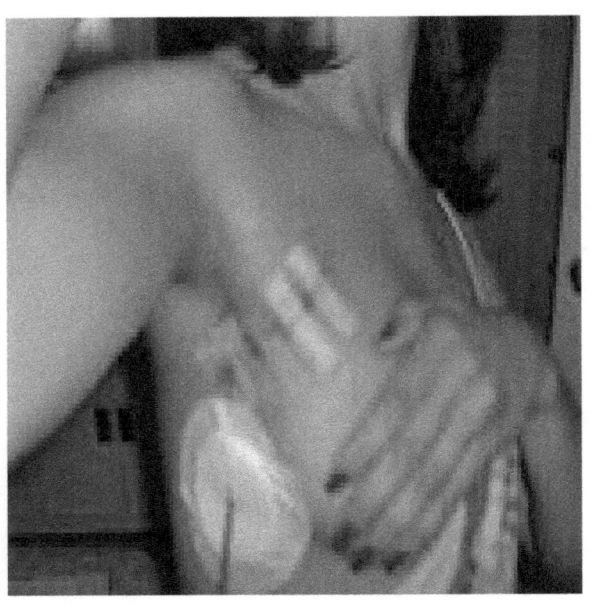

Post-lumpectomy-May 12, 2007

I was educated about lifestyle changes to avoid getting lymphedema, which is the accumulation of lymph in soft tissue with accompanying swelling, often of the extremities, sometimes caused by inflammation, obstruction, or removal of lymph channels. I should refrain from lifting anything heavy with the affected arm and should avoid needle sticks and blood pressure cuffs on that side. I should also carry a smaller handbag and close friends are quick to remind me of this!

As my arm became stiffer and the pain increased, I went online and researched cording. Cording has got to be one of the worse post-surgery complaints there is! It felt like a rubber band was under my arm and if I lifted it, it would snap. Dr. Marler's nurse told me to try and take my right arm over my head to touch my left ear. She might as well have told me to touch my nose with my tongue! I immediately got on the internet and researched the anticipated recovery time for an axillary lymph node dissection and return of range of motion which was expected to be 4-5 months. I was hoping for 4-5 weeks! Phil offered to help me stretch the arm and he would act as a physical therapist on most days; taking my arm and holding it in different angles. I can't stress enough how wonderful he has been during this ordeal. As he would massage the cording, I would bite my lip in pain but it had to be done. The cording must be broken up.

Friends and family started to make their rounds and I didn't want to look like how I felt on the inside so I put on my favorite bright yellow house dress and some matching gold eye shadow. Cancer doesn't have to rob you of your fashion sense! Phil and I had a tough battle ahead but I didn't have to always look sick. If you are on bed rest, you can still get up and put on your makeup if even just for you. It helps to have that glamorous face staring back at you in the mirror. Remember, half of winning the battle with cancer is your attitude.

My husband's family was very supportive when I came home from the hospital. His mother and sisters came over one weekend and cooked us enough food to last for several days and my girlfriend Twana also brought over a tray of "vittles" which included brisket, macaroni and cheese, baked beans and steamed vegetables. Phil and I were exhausted from the hospital stay and didn't have the energy to cook so thoughtful gestures like meals were greatly appreciated. I was beginning to feel guilty that I couldn't cook and I was tired of seeing Jackie and Phil sustain on fried chicken tenders and hamburgers!

Three days after my surgery, it was Mother's Day. Jackie painted my nails while I rested and Phil helped me with a bath using my new Bath & Body Works products he had given me. The pampering was a big boost to my mood and ego. It is very hard to bathe or even use the bathroom with the JP tube hanging out of you so feeling fresh was a welcomed state of mind. Taking a bath became a real task because the tubing couldn't get wet. It was also very awkward to sleep comfortably out of fear of pulling the tube out during the night. And remember that I was a newlywed? Intimacy went out the window too.

The Lortab medication seemed to take the edge out of the pain but it didn't knock me out as I expected. From my experience, I realized that you have to relax and give in to the drowsiness effect

Saltwater Taffy and Red High Heels

of the medicine. I found myself sleeping well when I got in the bed and relaxed rather than walking around like a busy bee doing housework waiting for the drowsiness to set in. The pain was becoming moderate. Most of the discomfort came from the itchiness and pulling of the lumpectomy site and underarm pain. Even Cotton seemed to want to help! He became even clingier than his normal state and would lie across my feet or stomach; rarely wanting to leave my side. I felt very fortunate to have this much love and support in my household. I just can't imagine anybody being on this journey alone. Even if you are an independent person who is reluctant to ask for help, now is the time to humble yourself and accept the kind gestures from those around you. Cancer brings out the best in others. Complete strangers would extend sincere and heartfelt hugs to me.

My neighbors were great; often stopping by to say hello, check in or deliver a little gift. I collect wall crosses and received several of them which provided reassurance that people were really praying for me or that they really observed my likes and dislikes.

Five days after the surgery, I was getting very frustrated. The incision site and stitches began to really irritate my sensitive skin and my physical activity and range of motion with the JP tube was greatly impaired. I also had a difficult time getting dressed since my range of motion was so impaired. When will the draining stop? It couldn't be removed until the fluid level was 30 cc or less for a 24-hour period and as of that morning; I was still draining at

Saltwater Taffy and Red High Heels

90 cc. It took everything in me not to pull the tube out, rip off the gauze pads and scratch the hell out of these stitches.

As my luck would have it, I was cast as an extra in "The Great Debaters" movie directed by Denzel Washington. Denzel Washington! Wow! Despite having the tubing, I was on the set for two weeks and hid the tube in my bra. The 14 hour days were exhausting and at times, I felt like I was about to collapse. But I signed up for this so I had to stand by my word. Several of the extras saw it while we were dressing and inquired about it. I was glad to share my story and wasn't ashamed of it. The registered nurse on the set was very accommodating and would help me change my dressing. She applauded me for being on the set and not letting the surgery or cancer get me down. And trust me, it would take a lot more than surgery to keep me from meeting Denzel. If you look closely at the beginning of the movie, I am seated next to Kimberly Elise's character in the church scene. I took great pride in my makeup and elaborate costume hair because I knew that having my hair styled was about to be a thing of the past for a long time.

Saltwater Taffy and Red High Heels

On the set of "The Great Debaters"-May 2007

Jaclyn threw herself into writing poetry and songs and dancing. She is a very talented hip-hop dancer and puts a lot of heart in her performance. Phil works in his music studio and produces beats or watches ESPN as a stress reliever. I know he misses going to the gym daily but he was reluctant to leave my side for very long. I could already tell that this experience was going to be a tremendous strain on everyone and I felt bad. Other times, I was very angry. This was my great life interrupted.

When all of the tape sutures finally fell off, I stood in the mirror and looked at the scar for about five minutes. I turned and looked at it from different angles. It wasn't as bad as I anticipated. It was actually a badge of courage.

Saltwater Taffy and Red High Heels

Chemo From Head to Toe

Dr. Marler was the first physician to utter the words CHEMO to me. When someone just says the words CHEMOTHERAPY, it feels like they are saying it in sloooooooow motion. It was almost surreal. I went from getting married, moving from Houston to Shreveport, seeing a doctor about a suspicious lump in my armpit and now I was faced with the possibility of losing all my hair? It was almost too much to fully take in. It isn't easy at all for a woman to accept the fact that she is going to lose her hair; even for medical reasons.

I was home alone during the day while Phil worked and Jackie attended school and probably doing way too much internet research about chemotherapy. I can't stress enough how terrified I was. I decided that I would forego chemotherapy and "live out my life to the highest quality." This was a dangerous thinking path because I was basically trying to say that I would rather die from cancer than fight the cancer and temporarily lose my hair.

I began to receive literature from various breast cancer support organizations and began seeing images of other young women who were battling or who have battled breast cancer. And you know what? They still looked beautiful bald. One young woman in particular really caught my eye one day at the cancer center. She was African-American and about my age and she was in the waiting area with her mother. To my dismay, she was bald and

48

Saltwater Taffy and Red High Heels

didn't wear a head covering. She had on great earrings and seemed confident and careless as to what people thought about her. I remember wishing that I had her courage. I wasn't there yet.

I always take my grandmother's phrases out of context and apply them to conveniently fit my situations. So my thoughts were nothing different when you called to say, "I have breast cancer and of my options, I may have to have chemo as well as have a lumpectomy". My thoughts immediately went to her catch phrase of "what doesn't come out in the wash, will come out in the rinse". Therefore, my logic was chemo would make everything all right. However, my logic was not your logic. During the course of our friendship, I'd never seen you so pessimistic about anything until you said "I'm not taking chemo, I'm just going to go with the flow. Let things happen as they may."

I initially said to myself "Did this girl just say she's not having chemo?" and you replied "I don't think it's worth it with all the side effects." Wow, you could've slapped me silly! Are you referring to your hair, your energy, your appetite, your social life? What are you referring to not being worth it? It was difficult for me
to accept that as a final answer, especially when I looked at Jackie, who adores and confides everything in her mother. Then Philip because I'd known him longer and for the first time, I was seeing him happier than he'd ever been. I knew that he was dying inside. I didn't think of myself as being selfish but instead thought that you were. I could only focus on how many lives your decision was affecting. Then your concerns finally hit home when one of my coworkers had to leave early because of feeling ill from chemo. I thought well this is Crystal's decision I should respect that and live with it.

I experienced a rollercoaster of emotions until you finally came to your senses. Did I think that chemo would save your life or

Saltwater Taffy and Red High Heels

prolong it? I don't know but I did think that the effects it would have on your quality of life didn't compare to chemo assisting in the longevity. My granny was right; it all came out in the rinse.

Mrs. Twana Jackson

I chose Dr. Joyce Feagin because I wanted a female oncologist. To my pleasant surprise, she was African-American. I had never had an African-American female physician before. Dr. Feagin sat down and blatantly asked me what I thought she was going to recommend. It was like she could read my mind because I was ready to verbally attack her and talk myself out of chemotherapy. She was readily prepared and showed me charts and medical documentation which supported that an aggressive six cycle round of chemotherapy would give me the greatest likelihood of a high 5 year survival rate. I found myself getting angry at Dr. Feagin but my anger was greatly misplaced. I was angry at what she was saying. I now have great respect for people in oncology because their jobs are very difficult and emotionally trying. As a patient, the news brought me to tears. I can only imagine how those who care for us must feel when they see lab reports and have to communicate that news to patients and their families.

Saltwater Taffy and Red High Heels

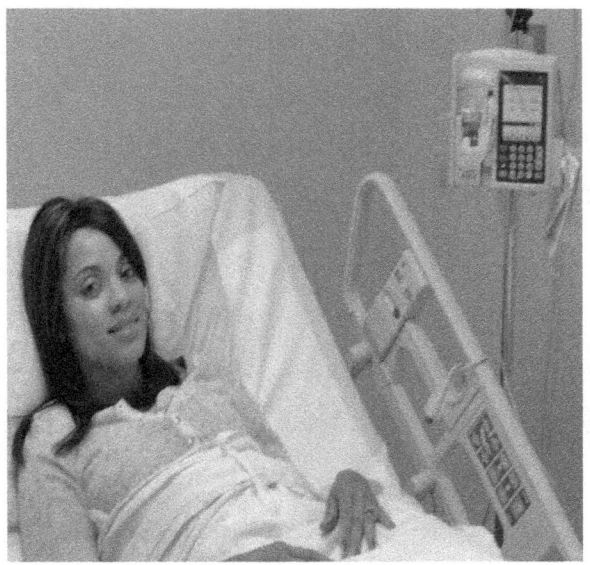

Me at my first chemo. (July 2007)

Images of chemo conjure up thoughts of baldness, being balled over in the bathroom hugging the toilet, toxins floating in your body and an overall sense of helplessness. My prescribed chemo cocktail would consist of taxotere, epirubicin and cytoxan administered every three weeks. I completed four of six recommended cycles. For very personal reasons, I opted out of the last two chemo cycles. I do not encourage not following your physician's orders but I made a well thought out decision which I felt was best for me.

The first chemo was the longest day at the center. I dressed comfortably and put on makeup in an attempt to psyche myself out. I wore a long wig so that I could get use to the idea of wearing it in public and to chemo. The first time that I took a tour of the

Saltwater Taffy and Red High Heels

chemo treatment area, I walked in, looked at all the rows of chairs and equipment filled with patients and immediately burst into tears. There was a pretty nurse named Shannon who appeared to have dropped everything and ran over to me. She took my hand in a soothing manner and talked me through it. That is what makes the difference in doing your job and being a wonderful employee. Shannon was reassuring and gently told me about the center. They found a chemo patient for me to meet and she was also an African-American female about my age. She was in a private room and had her teenaged daughter with her. They were watching television and laughing when I walked in. I asked her if the port hurt and she told me that she didn't even feel the chemo going in and that the process wasn't too bad. I thought "If she can do it, so can I."

I can not tell you how many times I tried to push the chemo date back. Looking back, I really didn't have a clear grasp of the timeliness and urgency to fight this cancer. I honestly thought I could start chemo in the fall when the weather was cooler and I had enjoyed the summer. At the first chemo, I had another wonderful nurse named Debbie who was thorough but gentle to all of my fears and questions. She explained every step of the process and every possible side effect. I was offered a menu of snacks and plenty of reading material. They did everything they could to make the day comfortable.

My private room had a television and comfortable bed. My husband, daughter, friends or mother-in-law would accompany me to chemo. I would wonder if it was hard for them to watch the "red devil" or epirubicin being administered. The drug is so powerful that the nurse has to actually sit at your bedside and manually push it into the vein or catheter. After the sedative and benadryl was administered, I would quickly fall asleep and wake up hungry. I think I ate more fried chicken and mashed potatoes than I needed to! My sister-in-law Karen sent us a large, beautiful basket of ham, bacon and pancake mix to promote that I eat a healthy breakfast on chemo days. I only threw up once as a result of the chemo and that was the first night after the first chemo. As I made my way to the bathroom, I asked myself if I had made the right decision. I couldn't imagine feeling this bad for a long time. I remember crying on the bathroom floor and being angry at God and the world. It was the most severe nausea I had ever experienced and had to take three different medications to minimize the symptoms. For future reference: chemo side effects were worse than natural childbirth!

I won't sugar coat it: chemotherapy is brutal. There are plenty of medications on the market to help you manage the symptoms but the overall experience was very difficult, uncomfortable, exhausting and downright depressing. Several times my white blood count was so low that I developed a condition called neutropenia and required immediate hospitalization. Do not pass Go and do not collect $200. Dr. Feagin didn't even let me go home and pack an overnight bag. One of my hospital stays was five days and I was miserable being cooped up in the hospital. I wanted to go home so bad but my Dr. cautioned me against the risk of any infection. I had to avoid small children, salad bars, fresh flowers, crowds, etc. I also received antibiotics and antifungals around the clock to fight off any infections. Phil would bring Jackie to the hospital and it hurt me so much to watch them go. Although a new stepparent, he was doing a wonderful job of taking care of Jackie. Sometimes when they left the hospital, I would cry because I was once again reminded that I was very sick and I missed the comfort of home. Now I understand why critically ill people desire to be home in their final days.

While researching chemotherapy on the internet, I looked hard for a book that would tell me exactly what to expect but failed to find one. Most of the books I found were outdated or written by older, Caucasian women. So I have broken it down, 2007 style, from head to toe:

Hair: I've dedicated a whole chapter to hair but I'll touch upon it here. Most chemo patients will lose their hair. I was naïve and thought that I would not lose my hair. It was just too long and thick and I had always had long flowing hair. Me without hair was like salt without pepper! During the third week after my first chemo, I began noticing that large chunks of hair were coming out and I noticed my hairline receding. I was in the shower one evening and noticed a bunch of hair on my washcloth. I called for Phil to come in and look at my pubic area which was now bald. It was a reality. The hair was coming out whether I liked it or not. My hair also became very dry and brittle and it wasn't the same texture. I made the decision to shave it and after I did it, hair loss was one less thing to worry about. Prior to shaving my head, my scalp began to hurt and became very tender with a tingling sensation. Even after shaving it, I would notice little hairs in the shower as if it was the root of the follicle. Rather than focus on the sadness of the situation, I reminded myself that the chemo was working. It was killing the cancer cells too.

Head: Throughout my twelve weeks of chemo, I had mild headaches which were relieved with over the counter medication. I have noticed that my memory isn't as good as it used to be. Some survivors call it "chemo brain." What is most frustrating is searching for the right words to say when I know the word but my mouth won't always immediately make the association. I can only hope that my recall comes back and I will once again be a confident and eloquent speaker.

Mouth: Eventually I did develop mouth sores and my mouth was very sensitive to hot and spicy foods. I had heard people talk about a metallic taste in their mouth but I really don't recall experiencing that. I can attest that some foods didn't taste the same and I preferred more salt and pepper than usual. In addition, my gums would bleed periodically and my teeth hurt mildly. The nurses gave me a recipe for a mouth rinse solution which provided me some comfort.

Bones: Twenty four hours after my chemo, I would have to return to the clinic for a Neulasta shot. Neulasta helps build up your white blood count which chemo depletes. The shot is mildly uncomfortable (I mean, who likes shots?) but the bone and joint pain I experienced was extremely painful. It brought back flashbacks of childbirth. The pain was so intense that I had to take a prescribed pain killer. Hot baths with Epsom salt also relieved my pain. I had to stop lifting weights as a result.

Fingers: After two chemo sessions, I developed neuropathy in my fingertips and toes. It wasn't painful; just a cold and buzzing feeling in my fingertips. At times, I would lose my grip on an object that I was holding. The symptoms subsided about one month after my last chemo.

Hot Flashes: These were the worst! I will never tell another menopause joke in my life. It felt like I was being plugged into an electrical outlet and many survivors will refer to these flashes as "power surges." I would be out in public and suddenly become so hot! I dressed in layers and always made sure to have a tank top as the last layer. I would wake up almost nightly in a sweaty panic mode and would often sleep with two fans on. They were that intense. My poor husband would be swaddled in blankets and here I was sleeping in my undies. I was prescribed Lexapro to combat the flashes and I personally didn't experience any benefit. Almost 6 months out from my last chemo, I no longer experience these "power surges" and have tapered off the Lexapro.

Stomach: The most embarrassing side effect was good ole' gas! I would try and avoid gas producing foods but it didn't help. My doctor said that chemo affects the cells in your stomach and suggested some over the counter medication. The gas continued until about 8 weeks from my last chemo. THANK GOD.

On days two and three after chemo, I would suffer from loss of appetite and nausea. The medication prescribed for these symptoms really helped but made me drowsy. The little weight I would lose on chemo weeks would quickly be regained during weeks two and three because when I felt better, I ate comfort foods to heighten my well-being.

Another side effect of the pain medication was constipation. No one really wants to tell you about this side effect but once you experience it, you will never forget! Think childbirth here. The best anecdote was increase of water and fiber....and plenty of good reading material in the bathroom!

Weight Gain: The thought of losing weight was ironically reassuring to me when I was undergoing chemo. I figured at the end of this journey, if I was thin and bald, I could live with that! Ha! I found that I had very little energy during chemo weeks and Phil didn't want me cooking if I didn't feel well. My sister-in-law Karen suggested stocking up on TV dinners. Duh! What a wonderful and obvious suggestion. I found that I could eat a variety of dinners and choose healthy options. Nutrition during chemo is something I highly encourage every breast cancer patient to research and try and commit to. Usually a nutritionist is part of your medical team as well. My doctor pointed out that most breast cancer patients actually gain weight as a result of treatment. Chemotherapy can slow down your metabolism. During the first few days post-chemo, I had very little appetite but when I started to feel better during the turn-around weeks, I ate lots of comfort food and barely exercised. At my highest weight, I weighed 169; 24 pounds heavier than my wedding day. I've since lost 13 pounds and am comfortable with my weight hovering around 150 pounds. I do drag myself to the gym at least 3 to 5 times a week and do 45 minutes of intense cardio and weight training. I remind myself that exercise is helpful in fighting recurrence. I've also adjusted my diet drastically and reduced sugar and empty calories. Cancer forced me to improve my nutrition and optimize my daily food intake.

Saltwater Taffy and Red High Heels

Nails: I am very thankful that I didn't lose my finger or toe nails. In fact, I would have been very distraught about that. I met a patient at the doctor's office who had lost her nails and they were black. They looked so bad that I wanted to cry for her. My nails did become brittle and developed white lines. My toe nails did eventually develop black spots which resembled a fungal infection. I avoided getting manicures and pedicures during chemo treatment to avoid the risk of infection. Almost 6 months out from my last chemo, my nails have returned to their normal state.

Skin: My skin turned an ashy, ugly grayish color. My doctor advised that my skin would turn darker which for me wasn't so bad. I like the way I look with a little sun but the color my skin turned was weird beyond description. It lacked a healthy tone but I would estimate that it returned to my pre-chemo state about 6-8 weeks out. It appears a little paler now and is clear of any blemishes.

Ovaries: I took the news that my ovaries may permanently shut down pretty hard. At my age (35), the likelihood of having a baby after chemo is minimal. As a newlywed, this was just too much to deal with. I stopped having my menstrual cycles into the second month of chemo and at six months out, I still don't have them. Now the truth is that I really don't miss them but I would welcome their return. Phil and I have discussed adoption if I am unable to have a baby. As much as I want to have a child with my husband, I have to face the reality that I may not be able to have another biological child. It seems selfish to put my own life ahead of a child but Phil gently reminds me that he can't love a baby that doesn't exist. He would rather have me here. It doesn't seem fair to him that the woman he married may not be able to have a child and that is just the harsh reality of cancer. (Good news update! While completing this manuscript, I did see a return of my period. Never thought I would be happy about having a period again!)

Scars: I honestly wasn't thrilled about the insertion of a catheter in my chest area to receive the chemo but the reality is that my veins could not handle the powerful medication. When Dr. Marler would go into detail about what the insertion would entail, I would once again become scared and try and think up reasons not to undergo the procedure. In the end, I overcome that fear. Plus, bruised and blown veins are not chic!

Once again, I went on the internet in search of information about the ports and came across a web site where an older gentleman talked in great detail with photos about his port-a-cath experience. He made it look so easy and he gave me the encouragement I needed. That is why it is so important for survivors to talk in great detail to other survivors about the journey. You can never fully be prepared for this experience but you can be encouraged.

The insertion surgery was done under anesthesia and I woke up to minimal pain. Because I am very thin up top (and only on top!) , the catheter stuck out more than I would have liked but it wasn't obtrusive. The first few days post surgery caused discomfort, which was relieved by placing a bag of frozen vegetables on the site, but within a few weeks, I adapted and often forgot it was there....or not. My OCD caused me to focus on it more than I needed to. Eventually, I got the courage to wear v-necks and scoop necks again without worrying about the appearance of the site.

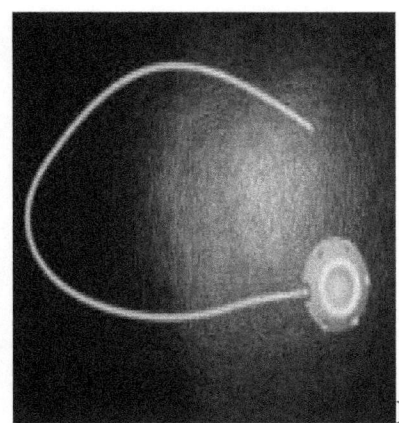
Photo of port-a-cath

The port was easy for the nurses to access and I applied a numbing cream over the area the morning of chemo days. Besides the initial stick discomfort, I didn't feel any pain or discomfort during chemo and looking around and seeing other people getting stuck in the vein repeatedly made me feel like I really made the right decision to get the port. When I completed chemo, I could not wait to have

Saltwater Taffy and Red High Heels

it removed. Thoughts of infection plagued my thoughts so I opted to have it taken out within the month despite Dr. Feagi's urging to leave it in. If I ever need it again, I will cross that bridge when I come to it. I mean, do you carry an umbrella everywhere on a sunny day?

The site hosts an ugly scar which is beginning to keloid. Although I am bummed out about the scar on a highly visible part of my chest, I try and not focus on it. I have a fellow American Heart Association lobbyist and friend named Molly who is a heart disease survivor. She proudly displays her scar from several heart surgeries which is pretty visible across her chest.

"I realized that my scar was a "tattoo" of strength and the visible sign of the blessing God gave me", Nolan says. Life is too short for me to be hung up on a little scar.

Saltwater Taffy and Red High Heels

<u>Hair Today, Gone Tomorrow!</u>

I'm going to get real shallow here. From the moment of my diagnosis, losing my hair has been one of my greatest concerns. Sure, Demi Moore and Natalie Portman shaved their heads for movie roles and managed to stay beautiful but I was no Hollywood starlet. The thought of losing my hair was absolutely terrifying to me.

I have always had long, thick, healthy hair. It is my security blanket and proud display of beauty for me. Long hair is a hot commodity in the African-American community validated by the extensive use of wigs, weaves, hair pieces and extensions. I have always taken GREAT pride in my all-natural, long, healthy mane. I had dyed it, flat ironed it, curled it, colored it, teased it, waved it, highlighted it, braided it, pressed it and put it into ponytails, buns and elegant up do's.

My hair at its longest. (circa 1997)

Saltwater Taffy and Red High Heels

One of the highlights of my life was being selected for a hair show sponsored by Dove and Conde Nast for Women's Entertainment television. I was one of four women chosen nationally for my "great" hair transformation. They flew me and a guest to New York City and we spent an entire day taping the nationally televised show. My hair was actually the winning component to this contest! The best part of the trip was meeting one of my closet friends, an attorney in Arizona, Margaret Lopez-Erpenbeck. Margaret is one of those rare people who you quickly want to make a life-long friend. In fact, she was a bridesmaid in my wedding and we email so often that she is my biggest confidante.

I remember when I bought my first wig. It was really hard on me emotionally because I have always hated anything fake-hair, nails, breasts, etc. For me, natural beauty is the way to go. Post chemo, as soon as I had enough hair that resembled hair, I took my wigs to the local American Cancer Society office.

Everything I read said to be prepared before the hair falls out because you just couldn't pinpoint it. I went to a local Asian owned beauty supply where a sweet young woman spent a good length of time with me while I tried on several styles. I felt silly initially with the wigs on my head but once I got used to the idea, it became fun to experiment with different styles. Now I know how A-list celebrities feel! As my good friend Linda joked, "Most Black women I know wear wigs anyway!"

Saltwater Taffy and Red High Heels

Since I needed to have fun with the wigs, I promptly named each one of them and wore them according to my daily mood.

"Donna"

"Meg"

"Rihanna"

Saltwater Taffy and Red High Heels

"Donna" was most like my real hair and my preferred look. It was a synthetic wig so I felt awkward wearing it without a hat or headband. "Meg" was a wavy style and was made of real hair and gave me the most natural look. "Rihanna" was the short, stylish, poised look that I always dreamed about. My mom actually picked it out for me. On days that I would get depressed about my hair, I would call the Y-Me hotline and speak to a survivor volunteer who would not only share her experience but would encourage me that I could get through this. They reassured me that my hair WOULD grow back in time.

One afternoon, I was shopping at a department store and was getting depressed about my hair. My friend Toni, who is also an author and client, kept me on the phone for about an hour and talked me in a stern but inspirational voice. She reminded me that what attracted me to her as a friend was my ability to persevere over challenges and my determination. She was seeing attributes in myself that I failed to see. Her pep talk still resounds in my head when I need some motivation.

I finally got the courage on July 20th, 2007 to shave my head. Having been inspired by so many courageous and strong survivors, I wanted to have the full experience and spare myself the daily agony of shedding, unhealthy and basically dead hair. Actually, my good friend Chef Tarsha Gary gave me the motivation I truly needed to accept that my hair was going to fall out. She first voiced the words to me-"embrace the full experience." It was a very empowering statement. Tarsha communicated that she knew I could weather this storm. I was driving home from the grocery store in what felt like 100+ degree weather when I was overwhelmed with a sense of strength. It was a do something now or never do it situation.

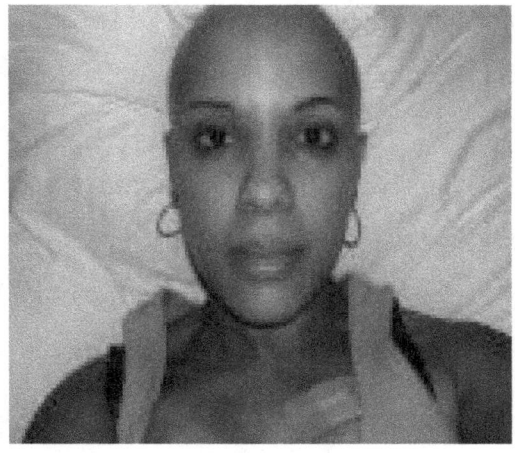

Self taken photo. I didn't look too happy.

It was such an important day in my life that I even recall what I was wearing! An Old Navy brand long linen skirt, chocolate brown tank top and my favorite leather sandals. I walked into the day spa, appropriately entitled My Spa, My Way and was promptly greeted. "I'm here to cut my hair off. My chemotherapy is causing it to fall out." The two greeters were surprised by my admission. They commented that I was beautiful and they had no idea I was even wearing a wig. The owner came out and took me to their private, curtained off area where a lovely stylist named Gina met me. As

Saltwater Taffy and Red High Heels

they lifted my matted hair, it practically melted in their hands. The owner suggested I go short to avoid the trauma but I had already made my mind up-I wanted to shave my hair off. I expected to completely loose it in the chair and cry uncontrollably but not once did I even want to cry. My hairline had begun to recede drastically and I wasn't happy with the hair texture or quality anymore. I just wanted to get over this mental hump about the hair. As she took the pink shaver to my head, I braced myself and squeezed the arms of the chair tightly. It actually felt good as the dead hair came out-that was cancer hair. When she finished, I looked in the mirror and smiled. I had done it! As silly as this may sound, I felt that I not only shed my hair that day but I shed a lot of insecurities and painful memories. I would be forced to learn how to love me-the real me not the made up me that meets society's definition of beautiful. I have to admit that I haven't been able to throw away the bag of my old hair. One day at a time. You can't get rid of the past overnight.

I was courageous that day and besides being bald didn't look that bad! Well, let me clarify that-I did not look bad bald! Ha!Ha! The stylist, Gina, was kind enough to style my wig that I wore into the spa. I walked out the same person as I walked in-just feeling more empowered and finally in control of this messed up situation! My best friend, Saleemah Jones, said that when she first saw my bald head in person, initially she was in shock. "I was used to seeing you with long, beautiful hair. After the initial shock wore off, I

Saltwater Taffy and Red High Heels

realized that the same loving and caring person I've known for years was still standing in front of me."

My family saw "Rush Hour 3" when it came out. To my surprise, the leading actress played by supermodel Noemie Lenoir, revealed a clean shaven bald head. And you know what, she was gorgeous! I was a bit taken aback when she took off her wig and went home and "googled" her to confirm that she did shave her head for the role. Women like her are strong and motivate other women to take their own beauty into their own hands.

In October of 2007, I decided to go on a local community affairs program entitled "Crossroads" which airs in Houston. But this would not be an ordinary breast cancer survivor piece: I would do the interview bald! The host of the show, Melanie Lawson, is someone whom I greatly admire and she is well regarded in Houston. Melanie went public with her own personal medical challenges several years ago and inspired me to be open and honest with television viewers.

I was quickly becoming a well-known entrepreneur in Houston and my face appeared in several magazines as well as being on the front page of the local newspaper. Since I had the name recognition, I felt that I could be a great spokesperson for breast cancer awareness. But what was really at the root of my desire to go on television bald was the inspiration that a newscaster in San Antonio provided. Her name is Leslie Mouton and she is also a breast cancer survivor. She was the brave anchor who went on-air

Saltwater Taffy and Red High Heels

bald and appeared on several national television shows including "Good Morning America", "20/20" and "Oprah". My mom was visiting from San Antonio and mentioned that there was a news anchor who went on-air bald. We went to the internet and I "googled" Leslie. What an amazing woman! She managed to capture her whole journey in a five minute video. I was able to see her transformation from the diagnosis to the healing. She actually looked better in my opinion with the short hair but what really touched my heart is how confident and secure she was. I emailed her and to my surprise, she immediately emailed me back. We communicated several times and I can honestly credit her for inspiring me to also go on-air bald. Sisters unite!

Speaking of sisters, I did the television interview on "Crossroads" with Karen Jackson, the CEO and Founder of Sisters Network (www.sistersnetworkinc.org). Sisters Network is the only national African American breast cancer survivorship organization in the U.S. In fact, Karen was one of the first people I reached out to after my diagnosis. I had been acquainted with her daughter, a successful magazine publisher, and familiar with her work in the breast cancer community. Karen was attentive and caring but also direct in educating me about my choices and cancer. She walked me through the pathology report which can be very intimidating for someone with no medical knowledge. It made me very proud when I would see Sisters Network listed as a resource on most of the literature I received from various cancer organizations because

Saltwater Taffy and Red High Heels

Sisters Network actually impacted my well being unlike other organizations who get the national name recognition but do nothing for its so-called constituents. Try getting their CEO on the phone!

In the Fall of 2007, I also appeared on a national talk show! I couldn't believe this opportunity had FINALLY arrived and I was now bald. Shoot! This particular talk show was my dream appearance and the timing was unbelievable. I took "Meg" and my actual friend Rhonda Nwosu with me. To my great relief, the other women on the show didn't know I was wearing a wig until I shared it with them. It took a lot of confidence to go on national television with a wig on but it was an opportunity that I couldn't pass. I had a compelling story that I wanted to share. It was also a once in a lifetime moment to meet one of the greatest talk show hosts of all time!

Rhonda and I had a fabulous time! A designer friend of mine and fellow Woman on the Move Award recipient Gayla Bentley, loaned us some stylish clothes from her collection to wear and we looked like a million bucks walking the streets of Chicago. Rhonda helped me put my best foot forward with exquisite jewelry and make-up and I was glad that I asked her to come along. I can't stress enough how much the love and support of a genuine friend can help you weather any storm.

I completed my last chemo on September 6, 2007. Shortly afterwards, I realized that my eyebrows had fallen out and I had two or three eyelashes on each eye. They were trying to hold on and I even put mascara on them so they could really stand out! I don't even recall losing them. I just woke up one morning and noticed they were gone. Now I began to get depressed. I could cover my head with a scarf or wig but I didn't really know how to create eyebrows and I felt like I was really beginning to look like an alien. I was reluctant to go out on many days because it began to take too much effort to put on my wig, adjust it, create eyebrows, etc.

About a week later, I was impatient for the hair to grow. I would wake up every morning and run to the mirror. Phil still likes to laugh at the two little grey V shaped hairs I initially had. Then the hair stubble was blonde. After two months, I finally saw new baby hair.

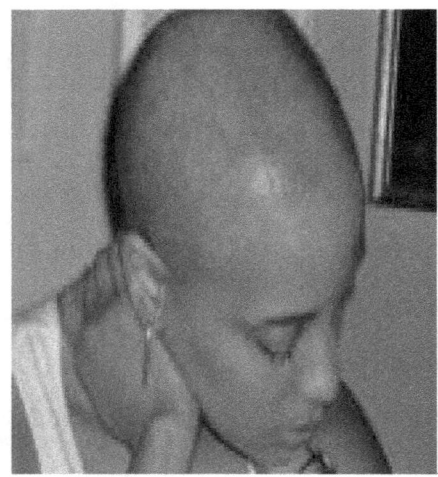Author at two months post-chemo

Saltwater Taffy and Red High Heels

The hair on my legs and lip grew back first. Oh and I think the hair on my big toe beat them to the punch! By the time this book is published, I expect to have about 6-8 months of hair growth. What was once an obsession in my life is now just an accessory. My hair doesn't define me. It doesn't make me pretty. It only covers the most valuable asset I have-my brain.

I had read where other survivors say that they received more compliments on their hair when it was short and I can testify to that claim. I now have a head full of curly hair (think poodle!) and get at least one compliment a day from total strangers on my hair. I am not certain if I will grow it back long again but I am embracing every stage of this and having fun with the new looks. Most of the time I will share my breast cancer story when someone comments on my hair but as time goes on, I am learning just to accept the compliment.

I had blonde highlights added about four months after the last chemo and I love it! I always wanted blonde highlights. Who knows? I may even get a pink streak along the way. Hair grows and some people don't. Always remember that.

Saltwater Taffy and Red High Heels

Me at four months post chemo-head full of hair again!

There are days that I get down about the loss of my long hair. I will see a shampoo commercial and wish for longer locks. I may flip through a fashion and beauty magazine and notice that most celebrities, even men, have long, flowing hair these days. But then, I think about why my hair is short and the feeling of sadness goes away. I'm still here! Nothing is better than that.

When I see other women with short hair or bald, I try not to stare but I do say a little silent prayer sometimes. I feel like I can spot someone on chemo a mile away. The urge is to go over and offer a hug or word of encouragement but you just can't approach all strangers like you used to. Who knows? Someone may have looked at me when I was bald and felt the same concern and sympathy. There were days that I was very self-conscious and insecure about my wig wearing but I began to notice how many OTHER women in my town wore wigs. Wigs and hair pieces are socially acceptable now. It is a fun way to change your look. I really don't think I will wear a full wig again unless it's Halloween but having been bald, I can truly appreciate just having hair on my head. I received so many compliments on my natural curly hair but I eventually tried to relax my hair again. The curls did not budge! You have to wear your hair as you want to. Many people will comment on the look they like for you but at the end of the day, you are charged with your own happiness. In any event, no more bad hair days for me ever again! It's all good.

Saltwater Taffy and Red High Heels

Goodness Radiates

Whoever says that "radiation is a piece of cake" must have been eating mud pie! Yes, chemo is like warfare and you feel indestructible after completing it but radiation was very hard on me mentally and physically. It was the day to day routine that wore on me.

My radiologist was Dr. Sanford Katz. Dr. Katz has a wonderful and patient (no pun intended) bedside manner and took plenty of time to explain radiation to me and Phil. He was also very patient when we bombarded him with so many questions. After the first office visit, I was sent to the clinic where I was marked up like a chalkboard with permanent marker. Just when I was beginning to get my self confidence back, I had to deal with another cosmetic blow. I just didn't like the way it looked. I was a walking maze! When they told me that I would have to stay marked up like this for the entire seven weeks, I was really bothered. The markings were visible in almost any type of shirt I wore. I just wanted my old body and self back. I knew the light was at the end of the tunnel but I still felt a sense of hopelessness.

Saltwater Taffy and Red High Heels

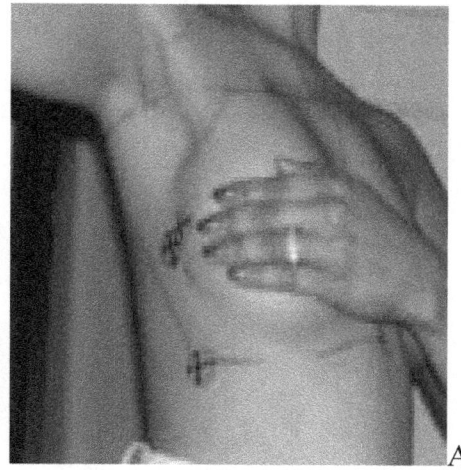
After first visit to radiologist

The markers helped keep me align with the radiation machine. Now lying on the table and receiving the radiation wasn't uncomfortable at all. The most challenging part was that I had to lie completely still and couldn't move at all. Not being able to move became a chore; especially during cold and flu season when I had sudden urges to cough, wheeze or sneeze. The technicians could fully monitor me from outside of the room. The initial awkwardness of lying bare chested in an open area quickly subsided because of the high level of professionalism exuded by the radiation staff. They see breasts everyday and mine were nothing to marvel over. I felt really vulnerable as women with headfulls of hair stood over me and adjusted my half naked body to line up correctly with the radiation beams.

What I found most frustrating was spending 30-45 minutes to get ready to drive to the center, undressing into the hospital robe and then lying on the table all of five minutes if that! I had 37 radiation treatments spread out over the weekday. For the most part, I drove myself and diligently counted down each treatment. Someone needs to invent a radiation chocolate advent calendar! They would make a million.

By the end of radiation, I was suffering from extreme fatigue. It was a fatigue that I have never known. I would be fine and then suddenly get so sleepy that I could barely function. I began to notice mild skin burning during the third week. About the fifth week, the radiation area was worse than a bad sunburn. The skin appeared to be dirty and had a black, ashy tone to it. My skin was so raw that I slept shirtless with my arm raised above my head and the ceiling fan blowing on it. Of course, there was ointment I was given to help but this was one bad burn.

Several months out of radiation, my skin has almost returned to the normal state. There is still a darker shadow over the area and slight evidence of the radiation marker imprint. The lingering feeling of exhaustion still exists and I just don't have the energy or strength I once had. I tried to jump back out there to my normal routine as if I never had chemo or radiation and that was an unrealistic approach. I realize now that my body is a machine and like all well-oiled machines, they should be turned off when not in use.

Although I got so tired of driving to the cancer center every weekday, I did manage to meet some of the nicest women I have ever met. When you are waiting in the radiation area, you meet other women who are on this journey with you. Some had breast cancer while others had brain and colon cancer. In my situation, I was one of the younger women and stood out. My fellow survivor sisters would ask me questions and comment on my age and express they were sorry that I was battling this at my age.

The older women had so much humor, wisdom and concern for me that I actually looked forward to seeing them daily. One woman named Barbara told me that she could tell how I was feeling by my choice to wear a wig that day or a scarf with no makeup. And boy was she right! On my "bad" days, I wouldn't put on a wig, make-up or dress up. Those velour jogging suits became my outfit of choice. There were days that I felt like I deserved a round of applause just for getting out of bed and you want me to put on make-up too? Please!

The radiation routine became so old but I knew I had to do it. I did miss a few appointments because I was just too tired to get out of bed and drive to the center. Once again, I honestly thought about quitting treatment but I knew I had to fight. Fight hard. I had come too far to give up.

On my last day of radiation, I surprised the radiation staff with cookies and sweets. They had all been so kind and professional that I could never repay them. As I heard the four series of beeps for the last time, I fought hard to fight back the tears. It was all over. It was really over. This day had finally come. I celebrated by going to my friend Sofia's holiday party and spending the weekend in Houston on my old stomping ground. It was time to kick up "my heels" and really celebrate. I also wanted to show off my new hair growth! Hopefully, I would never have to do surgery, chemotherapy or radiation ever again. But if I do, I am prepared and know what to expect.

Saltwater Taffy and Red High Heels

Angels Among Us

One of the best aspects of dealing with breast cancer is that you join a very special sisterhood whether you like it or not and the membership is irrevocable! Once two survivors meet and exchange stories, it is like an unspoken love and show of strength. You instantly have a spiritual connection and bond. Once you are fully on the survivor side, you have a deep level of sympathy and understanding for women who are still going through treatment.

I became aware of a nonprofit organization, Y-Me organization, which offers a 24-hour phone hotline to offer comfort and guidance to anyone who calls with a breast cancer diagnosis. The women who answer the hotline are volunteers and also are survivors. On the several occasions that I called, the women on the other line were helpful, understanding, nurturing and comforting to me in some of those darkest hours.

The Rose is Houston area's leading non-profit breast cancer organization providing mammography screening, diagnosis, early access to treatment and support to all women regardless of their ability to pay. Co-founder Dorothy Weston Gibbons and I had the honor of being named a Woman on the Move by Texas Executive Women. Through that association, we became email buddies and she was so supportive and nurturing during my initial diagnosis. One afternoon, I received a big care package from The Rose

Saltwater Taffy and Red High Heels

complete with a handmade quilt, baseball cap, informative literature and many other goodies.

There were days at the treatment center where I could tell that someone wasn't feeling well; other days I could see fellow cancer patients with a smile on their face. Everyone I met at the cancer center was warm and friendly despite the circumstances. There wasn't one visit where someone, perfect strangers, wouldn't look me in the eye and offer a warm smile or greeting. The best thing a person can offer someone going through chemo is to look them in the eye and speak to them directly just as if they weren't bald or sick.

One afternoon at the cancer center, I met a survivor named Lee Anne who offered friendship, courage and strength. Like myself, she was very talkative and outgoing. She sat on my hospital bed and shared her story with me. I marveled at her hair which now sat on her shoulders and was healthy and bouncy. I almost didn't believe her when she said she was completely bald just a year prior.

On August 13th, I had my one year check-up. I had planned on wearing something different that day, but decided at the last minute that I would wear pink, complete with my pink cap and tiara. It was a reminder for myself that just one short year earlier, I was bald and finishing up my treatments. During that time, my motto was, "On no hair days, you must wear a tiara!"
I went to the Cancer Center and met you in the lab for the first time. I thought you were such a beautiful vibrant woman. You smiled and commented on my tiara. I told you my story and you said that you had

Saltwater Taffy and Red High Heels

no hair. I had no idea. At that time, the nurses got busy working on me and you left. I saw you get in the elevator and I knew where you were going. I was hoping to see you again, just to talk to you. Then I saw you in the waiting room talking to the two elderly women. What a beautiful gesture you made by putting your arm around me and saying that "This is the lady I was talking about." Once again, we couldn't talk because we were both called back to our respective oncologists.

While waiting to see my doctor, I knew I needed to see you again and really wanted to talk to you. At that time, I had no idea that I would be giving you my tiara or my cap. I prayed, "Lord, if you want me to see her, make a way," and He did! I was walking down the hallway when I saw you and Jackie standing in the waiting room. I handed my paperwork to the nurse at the front desk and said I'd be right back. All I remember is that that room was filled with people, but it felt like the three of us were all alone. I knew then that the tiara and cap were no longer mine. I'll never forget the look on your face when I asked you to remove you wig. You were terrified. I said that no one here will mind. Jackie even said, "It will be fine Mom, take it off." I immediately slipped on the cap and tiara and the room broke out in applauds, cheers, and tears.

You asked for my name and address, which I gladly gave you, but not so you can give the tiara back. The tiara must be passed on. It has the power to open doors that a plain bald head does not. When people see someone with a bald head, they shy away, knowing the reason and not knowing what to say or do. The tiara makes the wearer approachable, allowing her to tell her story.

I wore my tiara to all of my treatments. On days when I felt incredibly bad, I even wore it. It made people smile. I may have felt like crap, but someone else who felt the same way I did had a chance to feel a little bit better for just a minute that day. That's the power that I gladly pass on to you! Wear it with pride my friend!

Ms. Lee Anne Bailey

When I shared Lee Anne's email with another survivor friend of mine, she had this to say:

Saltwater Taffy and Red High Heels

> *Crystal--this woman is your "live" message from God...you know that is how God speaks to us...through the "words" of others so that we can actually hear Him and not just wonder if the message we're imagining is real. You are loved. You are blessed. You are a "chosen" one. YOU ARE A SURVIVOR! When you next write to that new friend and messenger of God...please tell her she touched my heart as well.   Love, M*

I really thought that was nice of Lee Anne to give me her special tiara. I keep it in a special place to this day. She made me promise to "pass the tiara" on my one year anniversary mark. What is really inspiring is that her gesture sparked her imagination and dreams and she founded a nonprofit organization dedicated to giving tiaras to other women affected by hair loss. Of course, I will serve on the Board of Directors! We traveled to Dallas one day and volunteered with Brides Against Breast Cancer (BABC). The Executive Director donated more than 50 tiaras to our cause! BABC is part of the Making Memories Breast Cancer Foundation which grants wishes to women with stage 4 cancer.

Along with the tiara, I received a beautiful pair of crafted pink stone earrings from my friend Margaret.

The first thing I thought when I heard the news was - darnit, I wish I lived nearby! I would have driven on over and taken you out for a coffee and tried to lift your spirits in some way. Given that I do not live nearby, my next best alternative was to buy you a small gift to try and lift your spirits. I hoped that I was quick enough to surprise you - and that when you opened the gift, you'd get the same jolt that a mug of java would've given you had I lived nearby to offer that instead!

Saltwater Taffy and Red High Heels

I went online and googled the heck out of my gift - I wanted to make sure it was not only cute and thoughtful, but that it was appropriate given the circumstances and that a portion of the proceeds would benefit breast cancer. I found the gift, and while placing the order I mentioned the purpose for the gift. In addition to my cursory and automatic computer generated confirmations, I quickly received a personalized response from the owner of the site. When she read my order she wanted to let me know personally how nice she thought the gesture was, and what a good friend I was for you.

The earrings were hand made only upon my order, and a portion did go to benefit breast cancer. They were nice and pink, and I hope that when you got them your spirits were lifted momentarily by the unexpected surprise.

Mrs. Margaret Lopez-Erpenbeck

Although presents are always nice, there are so many other gifts that you can give to a woman on this journey. The gift of time is a beautiful one. Sometimes just spending time together can ease the pain and depression. I really enjoyed getting dressed up, slapping on the wig and going out with friends. You feel safe when you are with your friends. You don't worry as much about the wig or head covering because your friends have your back.

I really enjoyed receiving all of the greeting cards and notes. On days where I couldn't get out of bed or just plain refused to, when Philip would bring me the mail and there was a handwritten note, it brought cheer to my day. I saved every card that I received and when I re-read them, it reminds me that I am loved. I met a woman on E-bay named Judy who makes custom breast cancer stationary. We quickly became email buddies and she requested a card shower on my behalf. I received greeting cards from more than 30 women across the U.S. whom I had never met but we all shared the common experience of fighting breast cancer. I was deeply touched by the random acts of kindness.

Phil threw me a fun 1970's party for my 36th birthday. I had so much fun dancing the night away with my fellow hippies and soul patrol. For the moment, it felt like another birthday celebration. I didn't even think about the cancer.

My Houston girlfriends had met me for a birthday luncheon earlier that week at one of my favorite restaurants. It was wonderful to see them all again and most of them had not seen me since I started treatment. I had planned on wearing "Meg" at the luncheon but I just felt so uncomfortable sitting there with that wig on my head. Once again I'll say that I just don't care for anything fake and I don't like putting up a front. Besides it being so hot outside, everyone knew I was bald anyway! So, I decided to remove my wig and really feel comfortable. It is a blessing to have friends that you can be yourself around. I just can't stand anything fake or pretentious and wanted to let my guard down (since I couldn't let my hair down!)

Saltwater Taffy and Red High Heels

My friend Jacalyn and I on my 36th birthday.

It was a beautiful day last fall when Crystal gathered many of her friends for her annual birthday celebration. This year's birthday held a heightened sense of joy not only for Crystal but for all us in attendance. You see, Crystal was completing her fight against breast cancer after many weeks of chemotherapy. Her prognosis was positive. We were all very excited. When we all were settled around the table, Crystal began talking. I was stunned at her beauty and confidence as she began sharing with us her cancer journey. That day she was donning one of her snappy wigs that projected "I am a survivor, hear me roar." It was in that moment I knew she was going to take her wig off and off it came. The significance of her shedding it was seeing in action what mattered most in life and that was life itself. As I watched Crystal's face upon being freed of the wig, it was like witnessing transformation. She was so lit up, so strong, so confident, we were all touched and blessed to be in her presence. Crystal is a living testimonial of what it means to face adversity head on with style, grace and a little attitude.

Ms. Joanna Temple

Saltwater Taffy and Red High Heels

A Las Vegas designer and philanthropist by the name of Lana Fuchs did something extraordinary for me and twelve other breast cancer survivors. She sponsored an Emerald Dream Ball and after a nationwide search, I was fortunate to be one of the winners. The Emerald Dream experience was an all-expense paid vacation to Las Vegas for me and a guest and the week would end with a first class celebration in our honor on New Year's Eve at the Rio Hotel. I took my mother and we had a wonderful time. In addition to the quality time together, I got to meet twelve other strong women who had traveled on the same path that I had. After the first few days, we interacted like old friends sharing laughter, stories, tears and triumphs! Lana and her staff were very accommodating and treated us like royalty. We received spa packages, gift bags, custom chocolates, jewelry and show tickets. If that wasn't enough, Lana designed custom evening gowns for us to wear as we strolled down the red carpet with celebrities including Ian Zehring, Chris Judd, Omarosa and Melissa Gilbert.

Me and Lana at her Las Vegas home.

Saltwater Taffy and Red High Heels

Lana didn't have to do what she did. She sought out to change the lives of thirteen women and give them a week of pampering at her expense. The generosity of others is such a beautiful thing that shouldn't be taken for granted. I will always be grateful to Lana for her generosity and giving of herself in so many ways to others. She is one of those "powerhouse" women that once you meet, you never forget them.

Never once have I experienced anything as wonderful as the "Emerald Dream." It has been more than a month since I have returned home and I can still see and feel the smiles of all 13 beautiful women. We are all from different walks of life, come in different shapes and sizes and come in all shades of colors but we have one thing in common.....we are survivors! I am so glad that Lana Fuchs had a dream to help make breast cancer survivors feel good about themselves inside and out. They [The Fuchs] are very kind, considerate and giving.

Ms. Georgia Stafford

Saltwater Taffy and Red High Heels

Ups and Downs, Highs and Lows

You never truly move on from cancer. The possibility of recurrence always lurks around the corner. Sadly, while writing this book, several people I know have been diagnosed with a recurring cancer. I wonder when and if my time will come. Until them, I will maximize each day and each experience.

My scars are a daily reminder of how far I have come. You can put it out of sight and mind for the moment but you never forget what you have been through and how hard you had to fight on the journey.

Breast cancer brought out the goodness in others. It also brought out the worse in some people. I will leave that at that. As a cancer survivor, I need to focus on positive energy and dismiss anything that can contribute to stress or a dent in my well being. I need to choose my relationships and commitments very carefully. Rather than deal with drama, I am more likely to just brush my shoulders off and move on. I didn't fight the battle of my life to emerge back into the same wasteful cycles.

In my darkest hours, I would lie in bed and stare at the ceiling. I think I was in mild shock on a few occasions but never let anyone know. I would stare in the mirror and see a bald reflection, sallow skin, dark circles, and a tired soul. On the wall, there hung a vibrant, cheery wedding picture of me with a headful of hair in an

Saltwater Taffy and Red High Heels

elegant bun. Why had I been stripped of the only external beauty that I have ever known?

The answer is simple: My outer perceived beauty was not who I really was. I had a genuine spirit just fighting to come out. In order for me to grow, I had to know true sacrifice. In order to truly know God's power, I had to feel powerless.

Breast cancer was very hard on my new marriage. Wise married women have told me that all marriages have struggles; we just got ours in the beginning. I feel that we were robbed of our first year as blissful newlyweds. The timing couldn't be worse but a closer evaluation made me realize that the timing was perfect. Phil came into my life when I needed him most. He was the type of man who would stand by my side and be there with me the whole journey. Although I think I am a strong person, I don't think I could have done this alone. There were chemo days that I had to literally crawl around the house due to nausea.

Phil and I on our wedding day. (3/24/07)

Saltwater Taffy and Red High Heels

Phil prayed very hard during my battle. He is a dedicated Christian who prays every night on bended knee. In fact, that is one of the things that attracted me to him. In all my adult years, I had never seen a grown man take a bended knee to pray dutifully. He could help me grow spiritually; an area I had yet to develop.

So many friends and family sent us healing scriptures from Lakewood Church and we read them feverishly. I received seven copies of Dodie Osteen's book "Healed of Cancer" and several other books by Joel Osteen. If you haven't read Dodies's books, I highly suggest that you do for inspiration and hope. Here is a woman who was diagnosed with terminal cancer years ago and was miraculously healed.

My good friend Rhonda Nwosu arranged for me to pray with Dodie one morning at Lakewood Church in Houston. Author Barbara Harris ushered us to our special seating area and Dodie prayed with me and gave me a prayer cloth. I treasured that cloth and kept it under my pillow, in my bra and in my nightstand. There is power in prayer and Dodie is someone who I deeply consider to be anointed. Prior to my diagnosis, I was a wavering Christian. I believed in God but there were times in my past that I was angry at God for some of the tragedies and obstacles that I had faced.

As I grew in my faith, while at the lowest point of my life, I did find comfort in scripture. I surrounded myself with other believers who were living witnesses of God's miracles and healing power. I don't declare myself to be perfect but I am a changed person for the better and for those around me.

I commend my husband for dealing with this in an honorable fashion. I know that I had severe mood swings and often didn't seem myself. Once I completed treatment, I almost immediately started feeling better. It may be psychological but when you wake up and you are completely done with surgery, chemo and radiation, you feel reborn. You may want to cry and laugh at the same time at your last radiation. You have brand new baby hair. You re-enter the world as you know it with baby steps. This is your second chance at life. Live it to the fullest.

A good sense of humor really helped me deal with the treatment side effects. One afternoon, my daughter, husband and I were driving home. It was a beautiful afternoon and I let my window down to take in the fresh air. Whoosh! My wig flew off and into the backseat. I laughed so hard.

One of the funniest incidents occurred when my neighbor from across the street wanted to visit me in the hospital. I was registered under Brown-Tatum but apparently they had another patient with a very similar name in the hospital at the same time. My neighbor was transferred to the "other" Crystal and it was an older woman who was very ill. She sounded disoriented on the phone so my neighbor told her husband how bad "I" sounded and rushed to the hospital. She was directed to "Crystal's" room and when she entered, she saw the back of a person's head with grey hair and sticking straight up! She thought "Crystal is checking out of here" and then saw it was a White woman! Boy, we still laugh at that. Luckily, she finally found me after remembering my daughter's last name was Brown and deducted that maybe I used that last name.

During treatment, I was feeling ill often and was advised to avoid large crowds. As a result, I missed weddings, birthday parties and other special events. I hated to miss those functions but I told myself that I would be around for the next big bash. You can either laugh or cry during challenging times and I hope that you fill your heart with laughter.

Saltwater Taffy and Red High Heels

Reflections

We all have a story to tell. It's just a matter of finding your own voice. As I look back over how quickly the last year has passed, I realize how much I have grown as a person. I also realized that not everyone in my circle has grown; and that circle is getting smaller. I appreciate life more, don't take anything for granted, enjoy the simple things in life and I enjoy life to the fullest. Before being diagnosed, I was a work-aholic, self absorbed entrepreneur who was always "busy". Now I am busy living! I kept a beautiful home and bought beautiful "things" to make me happy or to "appear" happy but rarely sat back to enjoy the fruits of my labor. I had a stack of books that I kept to read but I never had time to read them. I had dusty yoga DVD's. It was a rare occasion that I truly relaxed. I also see the true beauty in others. Beauty isn't defined by magazines, a size 6 or the media. Beauty is knowing who you are and offering that beauty to the world around you. A woman's smile is beautiful. Everyone has something to offer whether it's a smile, a good joke, a thoughtful gesture, a warm drink or a hug. We are all so fortunate just to be alive and we should spend that time wisely. It is okay to be selective of how you spend your time and who you will spend it with. I had a colleague once who said that after her breast cancer recovery, she just didn't have the energy to be as socially active as she once was and that people got upset that she declined their invitation. Oh well…..if people can't understand that, they probably shouldn't be in your circle to begin with.

It amazes me how people would comment to me that I didn't look sick or that I didn't like I have cancer. It made me question "How should a cancer patient look?" I was well aware that I was young to be battling this disease when most of the other patients in the cancer center were much older but we all had the same common ailment-cancer. It doesn't discriminate. It doesn't care how rich you are, how pretty, how successful, or where you are in life.

Breast cancer wasn't my first serious medical challenge. At the age of 6 months, I was diagnosed with asthma. My asthma has gotten progressively worse as I have gotten older. I know what it feels like to be on the brink of death and gasping for your breath. For me, an asthma attack is just as scary as a cancer diagnosis. I now have a better grasp on how to avoid attacks and triggers and those same health and lifestyle changes can help me keep both diseases at bay.

As crazy as it sounds, cancer can really be a blessing. You learn how to fight for your life. You learn how to take optimal care of yourself. You prioritize your daily tasks. You see who is really in your corner. Most importantly, when faced with your own mortality, you truly learn how to live.

Phil and I were deeply moved by Robin Roberts decision to share her journey with breast cancer with the "Good Morning America" viewing audience. I think I empathized with her more because I

Saltwater Taffy and Red High Heels

was a little further on the path and knew what she was about to go through. The morning that the show broadcast her last chemo, Phil and I sat in the bed and both got choked up. He had been a fan of Robin since her ESPN days and I was a big GMA fan. She handled her treatments with humor, dignity, and strength. Every morning when I see her broadcast the show, I smile and am proud of her resilience.

Tomorrow is not guaranteed. But the promise of today is offered. I don't want to die from cancer but I don't want to live with regrets, missed moments, anger or revenge. In the midst of the storm, I stayed afloat because deep down, I knew that I would get through this. I knew that my hair would grow back. I knew that one day this would be in the past and a part of my history...NOT my history.

I am stronger than I ever could have imagined. My strength can make others weak. I think our deepest fear is truly realizing our capabilities and strengths because we've been conditioned to think small. Start thinking big today.

I never did wear those red high heels. In fact, they are in a box unworn in my closet. And I never bought anymore fattening salt water taffy. Funny, how I once thought that what I wore or ate would bring me comfort during the most troubling time. I do plan to wear those heels someday...maybe while chewing on some taffy. I will definitely wear them at my first book signing! But

Saltwater Taffy and Red High Heels

today, I take great comfort in just being here to share my journey with you. I hope you enjoyed the ride.

Saltwater Taffy and Red High Heels

About the Author

Mrs. Crystal Brown-Tatum is the CEO and President of Crystal Clear Communications- a Houston based advertising agency and public relations firm. The firm, founded in 2003, was ranked as a 2006 and 2007 "Top 25 Public Relations Firm and named the 4th Fastest Growing Woman Owned Businesses in Houston in 2007 by the Houston Business Journal.

Mrs. Brown-Tatum is a San Antonio native and Honors College graduate of The University of Houston with a B.A. in Radio-Television. She has completed post-graduate work in public relations and is the author of three poetry books, one nationally published fiction novel (Caramel and Cream) and completed an Honors College senior thesis on the overlooked effects of gangster rap music on male perception of women.

Mrs. Brown-Tatum has appeared on several local and national radio and television shows and has had more than 1000 editorials published including editorial work featured in Vogue, People, Self, Shape, Elle, Today's Christian Woman, The San Antonio Informer, Houston Style Magazine and The Houston Chronicle. In addition, she is a features writer for the Shreveport Times and has appeared on Women's Entertainment Television as a featured guest on the Dove/Conde Nast "A Cut Above: Beautiful Hair" television show. Ebony Magazine selected her as a 2006 Top Bachelorette.

She was twice voted Miss Congeniality in the Miss Texas USA pageant and was a top ten finalist in the Miss San Antonio USA pageant. She was the first African-American women to be crowned Sigma Chi Fraternity Fight Night Queen. In addition, Mrs. Brown-Tatum was a recipient of the 2005 Emerging-10 award sponsored by the Houston Minority Business Council, a 2006 Women on the Move recipient and H Texas magazine named her a Top

Saltwater Taffy and Red High Heels

Professional on the Fast Track for 2006 and 2007. She also received a Texas Senate Commendation for her community service and was awarded a Distinguished Achievement Award from the City of San Antonio Martin Luther King, Jr. Commission.

Mrs. Brown-Tatum is also a highly sought out speaker on the topic varying from depression, advanced communication skills to business etiquette. She is a member of Sigma Gamma Rho Sorority. Mrs. Brown-Tatum is married to Sergeant First Class Philip Tatum and has one daughter, Jaclyn.

She may be reached at cbrown5530@aol.com or at www.saltwatertaffyandredhighheels.com.

"Finish each day and be done with it. You have done what you could; some blunders and absurdities crept in---forget them as soon as you can. Tomorrow is a new day. You shall begin it well and serenely, and with too high a spirit to be encumbered with your old mistakes and nonsense."   Ralph Waldo Emerson

Saltwater Taffy and Red High Heels

www.ingramcontent.com/pod-product-compliance
Lightning Source LLC
Chambersburg PA
CBHW051707040426
42446CB00008B/755